STURGIS STORIES

Celebrating the People of the World's Largest Motorcycle Rally

Text and Photographs by Thomas G. Endres, Ph.D.

Kirk House Publishers
Minneapolis, Minnesota

STURGIS STORIES

Celebrating the People of the World's Largest Motorcycle Rally
Text and Photographs by Thomas G. Endres

Library of Congress Cataloging-in-Publication Data

Endres, Thomas G.

Sturgis stories : celebrating the people of the world's largest motorcycle rally / text and photographs by Thomas G. Endres

p. cm.

ISBN 1-886513-66-X

1. Sturgis Rally & Races, S.D. 2. Motorcycling--South Dakota--Sturgis. 3. Motorcyclists--United States--Biography. 4. Motorcyclists--United States--Social life and customs. 5. Sturgis (S.D.)--Social life and customs. I. Title.

GV1060.147S7 E53 2002
796.7'5'09783--dc21

2002019800

Kirk House Publishers, PO Box 390759, Minneapolis, MN 55439
www.kirkhouse.com
Manufactured in the United States of America

Dedicated to
Everyday Heroes
Everywhere

Contents

Acknowledgments

I believe this book has been lurking around inside me for a long time, just waiting to come out. Just because all those pieces were rattling around in my brain, however, is not enough to create a book. The efforts of many people and organizations - in addition to a lot of help from the Lord above - are necessary to pull something like this off, and I'd like to take just a moment to thank them.

Thank you to the University of St. Thomas Faculty Development committee, for approving and funding a major portion of this endeavor.

Thank you to my many professional colleagues who have supported this project, particularly the faculty and staff of the UST Communication Department. Special thanks to Steve and Kathy Olsen for, both physically and intellectually, traveling along.

Thank you to all the friends and family members who have also supported this work from day one. Mom, Ray, Todd and family–you in particular are my strength.

Thank you to the great folks at Kirk House Publishers. Special thanks to Leonard Flachman, for having the foresight and faith to pursue this vision, and to Jesse Hubbard, for his creativity in putting the vision down on paper.

Thank you to all those who participated in the interviews. This book, obviously, would not exist without your willingness to share your stories. I pray I have done you justice.

And (can the words "Thank you" ever be enough?) thank you to my lovely wife and daughters. To my life and fellow-riding partner, Deb, thank you for coming downstairs after proofreading the introduction, and enthusiastically proclaiming, "This is great stuff!" Until that point, I wasn't sure. And to Krystal, Carleen, and Kellsie, thank you for coming along on that momentous journey, and for cheering me on around the dining room table and basement computer as I plugged away at its completion. Because of you, I am the richest man in the world.

Forward

By Ann Ferrar
Author, *Hear Me Roar*

Like the Great Wall of China, that long, gleaming, densely packed line of motorcycles on Main Street is probably visible from outer space. Yet the people riding those bikes are among the most down-to-earth you'll ever meet. That is the essence of rally week, when every August, the little town of Sturgis, South Dakota, morphs into a Woodstock-on-wheels. And that is the essence of Tom Endres' book, in which you are about to immerse yourself.

For many people, being at Sturgis during the Black Hills Motor Classic is a life-changing experience, one of those stunning encounters that gets imprinted in your brain and will never fade from memory: "Someday I'll tell my grandchildren about this." It happened to me. I was there for the event's 50th anniversary in 1990, steeping myself in the history, the mystique and adventure of motorcycling. I came back so inspired by the stories I heard, I embarked upon a journey of writing and riding that led to the book *Hear Me Roar*. Since then, the rally's 60th birthday has come and gone, but unlike drive-in theaters and roadside dinosaurs on Route 66, the annual American tradition that takes place at Sturgis shows no signs of becoming obsolete.

When the bikers descend upon this town, it becomes a microcosm of humanity, at once diverse and so strikingly similar. The superficial similarities have become a source of humor (thousands of men with beards and black T-shirts … OK, my husband fits this description, too). But the deeper common bonds are a source of inspiration, even comfort, because they exist and they thrive within the diverse cliques.

Where else can you spot a burly guy who looks like Grandma's nightmare image of an "outlaw biker," and then, a few feet away, Grandma herself? She looks like any nice old gal you'd see at the supermarket – except she's astride her own big twin, and she can tell you true stories of how she rode a hardtail way back in the 1940s when rubber and gas and cars were scarce in wartime. And, oh, did I tell you that the burly guy is really an accountant who has a family and wears a suit during the week?

Funny, no one bats an eyelash that people from all walks of life attend baseball games, or play golf. Yet outsiders marvel that people from all walks of life ride motorcycles and go to Sturgis. This is ironic, because the idea of going there is to shed your everyday life, at least for the week. Even the late billionaire Malcolm Forbes enjoyed slumming around Sturgis, smiling, shaking hands with the proletariat, and taking flight in his giant, Harley-shaped hot-air balloon.

Shakespeare said that all the world is a stage, and there are few more colorful stages than Sturgis during rally week. Here, the players are in full costume, in character, and for real, 24/7. There are bonafide outlaw bikers, both male and female. For better or worse, they stick to themselves, or so it's said. (I'll bet you didn't know that outlaw clubs have "goodwill" ambassadors – you'll meet one in these pages.) The drag racers and dirt-trackers are covered from head to foot in protective gear and they live to hone their craft ... the women and girls who "just want to have fun" are hardly covered at all; the trophies they seek are for coleslaw wrestling and the biggest weenie bite. The shadetree mechanics kick tires with their cronies, the vintage and custom-bike aficionados polish their bikes till the chrome wears off. The posers want to cruise and be seen and the tourists on their full-dress rigs are a willing and captive audience. And for the diehard adventure riders on their well-worn machines, Sturgis is a pit-stop for camaraderie during the latest long ride.

At Sturgis, the biker soul is bared, and here, you will see how motorcycling pervades that soul. So many bikers have a need to meld their love of motorcycling into other aspects of their lives that carry great meaning to them. It's not enough just to be a Vietnam vet and belong to that storied fraternity; you've got to ride with a veterans club. It's not enough to be Christian and share your spirituality with your congregation; you've got to ride with like-minded folks.

In stories and photographs of eloquent simplicity, Tom Endres' book celebrates the people – the bikers – who make it all happen. Storytelling is an ancient and revered art form that predates the written word. In this sophisticated age, still we are drawn to people's true stories – the number of biography magazines and documentary TV programs are a testament to our fascination with ourselves. Magazines chronicling both high and popular culture are filled with non-fiction profiles of interesting people, where fame is not a prerequisite, but eccentricity is. You may not have heard of the people in *Sturgis Stories*, but you will be equally drawn into their world, to the quirky biker subculture, and to their open, honest, straight-from-the-heart stories that Tom has captured within these pages. And someday, you will show them to your grandchildren.

Ann Ferrar
Author, *Hear Me Roar*

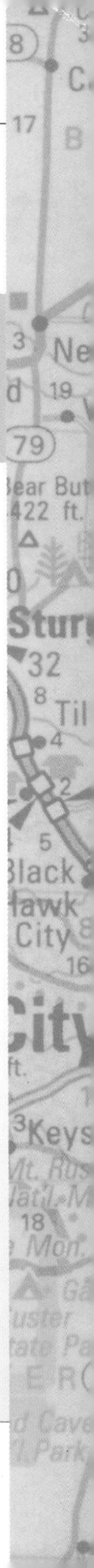

Author photo by Debra Endres

INTRODUCTION

No words can do it justice. Unless you have been to the Black Hills of South Dakota during the annual Sturgis motorcycle rally, you cannot understand what it is like to drive down the highway and be surrounded, completely surrounded, by hundreds of motorcycles traveling in both directions. The air literally vibrates with the sound, and your senses start to rebel at the overwhelming visual display. How can there be that many motorcycles? Where do they all come from? When you arrive on Main Street it dawns on you that you have only seen the tip of the iceberg. Those hundreds of motorcycles roaring by you on the roads were simply a warm-up to the thousands – no, the tens of thousands – of iron horses that are parked or parading up and down the six block main drag.

It is rally week in Sturgis. Variously named over the years – "The Sturgis Motorcycle Rally," "The Black Hills Motor Classic," and so on – the only thing that matters is this: It is rally week in Sturgis. For approximately ten days each August, the normally peaceful town of roughly 7,000 people transforms itself into a motorcycle Mecca. Leather-clad congregants from around the world make a pilgrimage to this, the granddaddy of all rallies. In some respects, Sturgis is like any other rally you might find in Daytona, Reno, or places thereabouts. Author Ann Ferrar paints a vivid picture of what these events are like: "Motorcycle rallies are places where the sport's subcultures mingle. They are ad hoc cities – gatherings of tribes where motorcyclists from all rides of life are brought together by their passion for two-wheeled travel. The larger rallies are fun, fascinating panoramas of all the strata within the motorcycle community. They are places for tire kicking, camaraderie, and, of course, riding."[1]

Even though you can do all those things at Laconia, Hollister, Humboldt, and so on, nothing compares to the history, heritage, and mystique of the Sturgis rally. From it's humble beginning in 1938, when Clarence "Pappy" Hoel and the Jackpine Gypsies Motorcycle Club hosted drag races for approximately 200 riders, to the record breaking crowd estimated at approximately 700,000 in the year 2000, the Sturgis rally has infused itself into the public consciousness. Ironically, the rally - and what goes on there - is often misunderstood or misrepresented.

Part of this misunderstanding stems from a reputation the rally earned for itself during the 1960's through the 1980's. The small crowds of dirt bike racers, who enjoyed free picnics in the city park, gave way to a rougher and rowdier crowd – the outlaw gangs. Gonzo journalist Hunter S. Thompson attempted to portray that era in his chronicle of the Hell's Angels. He is most quoted for his opinion that "the 'motorcycle outlaw' was as uniquely American as jazz." Most leave the quotation at that, and fail to follow up with his astute observation regarding the popularity of this self-proclaimed 1% of the population that lives outside the law. "Nothing like them had ever existed," Thompson argued. "In some ways they appeared to be kind of a half-breed anachronism, a human hangover from the era of the Wild West. Yet in other ways they were as new as television."[2]

While Thompson shed some insight into the outlaw phenomenon, it is nothing compared to the stories you can get from the outlaws themselves. In his recently published autobiography, Hell's Angels president Sonny Barger describes his experience coming to the Sturgis rally in 1982:

I was riding at the front of the entire pack and felt as if no power could stop us. It was like I became Chief Crazy Horse leading the charge with hundreds and hundreds of motorcycles all going eighty miles an hour. People in the towns heard the roar of our bikes way before they even saw us. The local police just looked the other way; 'Closed' signs flipped over on the merchants' windows as they locked their doors; mothers grabbed their babies from their yards and ran into their houses. Cars swerved over to the side of the road. But others, like the farmers, took off their caps and put them to their hearts and chests, and the local fire departments saluted us.[3]

Once they arrived in town, Sonny and company essentially took over.

We pulled into Sturgis, got off our bikes, and walked into town, strapped and tall. There were over fifty thousand bike riders in town that day, and the mood was dark and brooding. People sensed the Hell's Angels were there for a purpose. The crowd was quiet, and as we walked down the street it opened up like the Red Sea.... Fifty thousand bike riders weren't about to mess with four hundred Hell's Angels.[4]

But, as the saying goes, that was then and this is now. Sure, Sonny still rides, and the Hell's Angels and other outlaw clubs still come into town, but today's Sturgis bears little resemblance to those moodier days. The main difference is that the crowd of fifty thousand that Barger confronted has now increased tenfold, and most of those newcomers are not 1%'ers. They are 99%'ers. Renowned cultural critic and motorcyclist Brock Yates describes – in not very positive terms - the change that had taken place.

Here were the multitudes of boomers who'd dodged Vietnam in graduate school protractions, who'd considered high-risk living to involve the fat content in pasta, who were haunted by threats of asbestos, holes in the ozone layer, and the weak door latches in their minivans, suddenly pitching away their Perriers and their Birkenstocks and heading for the mad adventure of the open road. Freedom. Emancipation from middle-class guilt. Shredding convention! By God, here come the yuppie outlaws![5]

Yes, it's the "Yuppies." Or the "RUB's" (Rich Urban Bikers). Or the "Wanna-be's." Or the "Posers." Well, sticks and stones won't change the fact that Sturgis has a new demographic flavor. Each and every year, more and more older and wealthier individuals take up motorcycling as a hobby. According to the New York Times, the average owner of a Harley-Davidson these days is age 45, up from 38 just ten years ago. One in five Harley owners is 55 or older. And, as the Times points out, "Two-wheeled freedom does not come cheap."[6] Many of those older riders come from well established professional backgrounds.

As the face of the American motorcycle rider changes, so too does the face of the Sturgis rally. This is a positive thing. Change is inevitable, and all active systems – like a motorcycle rally – must grow in order to survive. The good news is this. When the new population arrives at the Sturgis city limits, they generally leave their pinstriped suits and power ties at the door (though many a saddlebag no doubt has a Palm Pilot or cell phone tucked within). Yates, who earlier ridiculed the Yuppie interloper, does admit the following: "Much has been done to sanitize the sport for public consumption, but at the core lies the renegade lifestyle."[7] In other words, whether real or wanna-be's, everybody who rides a motorcycle has to tip their hats (or helmets, or head wraps) to their forebears - the outlaws. Sturgis is about the leather, the look, and the life of the original hardcore motorcycling clubs. It may be temporary for some, but it is heartfelt. At the least, imitation is the sincerest form of flattery. Sonny Barger's days of bringing the town to it's knees in fear may be long gone, but everybody still gets on their knees (figuratively speaking) in homage to the image he and his comrades conveyed.

Such is the Sturgis that I wanted to capture in this book. The Sturgis that lies at the crossroads between its checkered past and its ever-expanding future. The Sturgis of today. The interviews for this book were conducted at the 2001 rally, though the specific year doesn't really matter. This could just as easily represent any of the modern day rallies from 1990 and beyond; the imprint of the era is so unmistakable.

Once I selected this as my goal, it was time to do a little soul-searching. I am not a biographer. I am not a photographer.[8] So what am I doing trying to create a book such as this? Well, I am a college professor who does a lot of research and writing. Mostly I study cultures and communities, which is exactly what Sturgis is. More important, I am a motorcyclist, and that's what it's all about. I conducted these interviews from the back of my classic 1980 Harley-Davidson Sportster XLH 1000. Granted, I sometimes thought the old Ironhead Sporty was going to shake apart my recording equipment as I tooled into town every morning, but all worked out well.

In the pages that follow, you will meet a cross-section of people who attended the 2001 rally. I was very interested in just letting them talk. Rather than be too directive, I wanted them to let me know what it was we should know about them. These are their stories. Just as oil and gasoline are the fluids that keep our bikes running, stories are the lifeblood of a community. These people's stories are the soul of the Sturgis rally.

Some talked about their jobs, their spouses, and their children. For others, those were the very things that they had traveled to the rally to get away from. Regardless of the starting point, conversation eventually and inevitably turned to several recurring themes and topics.

Topic number one: The weather. Yeah, I know, it's lame to talk about the weather. But during the 2001 rally, the temperature was over 110 degrees each day. A friend of mine's external thermometer on his car (which he swears is accurate) once read 126 degrees. It's hard not to at least mention the weather on days like that.

Topic number two: The crowds. The 2001 rally was not as big as the previous year (2000 had the honor of being the first gathering of the millennium, and the 60th anniversary of the rally itself). Still, estimates for the rally were coming in at approximately 400,000, give or take a few. Sturgis-Rally.com, the rally's official website, provides some additional statistics which give clues to just how large the event really is. 108 marriage licenses were issued. There were 880 vendor licenses. Six deaths. Taxable sales were over $11.6 million, and 436,800 tons of garbage were hauled. That's a big party.

When you talk about the crowd, you also have to talk about who makes up the crowd. Almost everyone has an opinion on the changing demographics, and the increase of older and wealthier riders. Some positive, some negative, most neutral – but everybody had something to say.

Topic number three: Women. One thing you will notice as you thumb through these pages is that there is not a lot of skin. Some, but not a lot. This is another misunderstanding about the rally. The public at large, when they encounter anything about Sturgis, hear it usually in television documentaries broadcasting images of women with digital mosaics blurring our view of their exposed breasts. A quick review of the few available videos and many available websites about the Sturgis rally are filled with images of those same flashing women (though generally without the pixilated censorship).

Sure that stuff goes on. All over the place. But there really is more to the rally than that. When you have a half-million people gathered together, you must understand that the stereotypes propagated in the media simply cannot describe everyone. To assume that every male in Sturgis has a rap sheet, or that every female wants to bare her breasts to anybody willing to look, is like assuming that every single person on the Las Vegas strip is either a headliner or a showgirl, or that each individual who walks through a turnstile at Disneyworld is dressed as a cartoon character. Sure, there are those who are entertainers. But a majority are entertainees.

On the topic of women, a more interesting question than, "Will you show me your breasts?" is "Do you ride your own motorcycle?" A number of women argue quite well why they prefer to be passengers, while others make it clear that riding their own bike is an essential part of the Sturgis experience. In her important and fascinating book, *Hear Me Roar: Women, Motorcycles, and the Rapture of the Road*, (a book idea conceived while she was riding from Mount Rushmore to Sturgis) Ann Ferrar makes the following claim. "When a woman masters a motorcycle, often she undergoes a change that spreads to other aspects of her life… When they learn to control a motorcycle, they do likewise with their fate."[9] This book has some wonderful stories of women who have their destiny, like their handlebars, well in hand.

Topic number four: Motorcycles. This seems obvious, of course, though I tried to veer away from the subject a little bit. This is not a book about motorcycles. It is a book about the people that ride them. Still, trying to interview someone over the roar of two or three thousand big-twin engines – well, it's hard to ignore.

You see a pattern in these interviews that is a reflection of what you see on the streets of Sturgis. The brand of motorcycles that people ride goes something like this: Harley, Honda, Harley, Harley, Kawasaki, Harley, Harley, Yamaha, Harley, Harley, Harley, Harley. You get the picture. Now, Sturgis is not exactly a Harley-Davidson only event. No one is run out of town (anymore) for riding a Japanese bike, but they are a definite minority. In Sturgis, Harley rules. And why not? As Brock Yates describes the increasingly popular trademark, he acknowledges that there "is something so elemental, so lusty, so purely and classically American about the machine that it is hard to resist"[10]. And Sturgis, South Dakota, he claims, is the "epicenter of the Harley-Davidson mystique."[11]

It is not surprising that the demographic changes and exponential growth at the Sturgis rally coincides with a parallel growth in sales at Harley-Davidson. For example, retired H-D CEO Rich Teerlink and consultant Lee Ozley observed that, in 1997, "Harley had racked up its twelfth consecutive year of record revenues and earnings. It had produced and sold more motorcycles than in any previous year in history. One hundred dollars invested in Harley stock in 1986 was worth slightly more than $7,000 by the end of 1998."[12] That level of production continues today. All those Harleys. Gotta ride them someplace. Might as well be Sturgis.

On a lesser note, a sub-theme often emerged in the motorcycle dialogue. It seems both positive and negative opinions abound regarding sport bikes, the lighter and faster motorcycle style – generally ridden by the younger crowd – which requires the rider to lay forward on the gas tank. Many refer to these bikes as "crotch rockets" (others refer to them more morbidly as "donor cycles," because of the high fatality rate associated with sport bike accidents). Look for those conversations as well.

Along with weather, crowds, women, and motorcycles, a potpourri of miscellaneous topics cropped up throughout the interviews. Drugs. Guns. College. Tattoos. Massages. Marriage. Jesus. It's all here. But there was something else as well. As I talked to all these people from different walks of life, different ages, different bikes, different backgrounds, I couldn't help but feel that there was some larger elemental force connecting us. I needed to push to find that common denominator. Yes, we were all in Sturgis together, but that wasn't all of it. There was more. Hmmm, we were in Sturgis because we rode motorcycles – so were "motorcycles" the force that drew us together? Close, but still not it.

I needed to ask myself the more foundational question. "Why do we ride motorcycles?" The answer is as simple as it is profound. It's freedom. The reason we were all there was our unshakeable belief in and desire for freedom. It starts with that personal sense of autonomy and control each individual biker has as they ride. Author, documentary director, and Harley-Davidson enthusiast Garry Garripoli describes the feeling beautifully. "The ride is a rush. You are so completely consumed that you are free from the trappings of life. No financial pressures, no relationship hassles, no responsibilities. You grab hold of both handgrips and at once let go of everything you left behind. The noise is louder on your bike, but it is still. The roadway pounds and the hours strain at your flesh though you are comforted."[13]

That definition of freedom is wonderful, but when you multiply it by the thousands and thousands of people at the Sturgis rally, it is somewhat incomplete. It looks only at freedom for the individual, and not the community at large. Garripoli later provides another definition, a Taoist definition, that stems from his expertise in Chinese medicine and Eastern healing. He equates freedom with acceptance. "To be free, you must be able to accept things and people for what and who they are. It doesn't mean you have to like them or even agree with them. It just means you don't change who you are because of them."[14]

That is the essence of *Sturgis Stories* – the freedom that comes with acceptance. The privilege of individuality counterbalanced with the responsibility of treating others different from yourself with civility. No matter what you ride. No matter what you wear (or do not wear). Regardless of your age, sex, skin color, affiliation, or income, you can only be for freedom to the extent you respect and defend other people's choices as much as you do your own. And this freedom represents something terrifically important. This freedom represents nothing less than America. To me, it boils down to the following elementary equation.

Sturgis means Motorcycles. Motorcycles are Freedom. Freedom is America.

Like everyone in the free world, I was shocked and horrified by the terrorist attacks on the United States, September 11, 2001. It was a month to the day since I completed my last interview, and I was still in the process of typing the transcripts. Like so many others, I reevaluated and took stock of my life. Was what I was doing important? Given the tragedy in the world, was I helping to make a difference?

Happily, I concluded that I was. This is an important project. The Sturgis motorcycle rally is a unique slice of Americana. Nothing identical to it exists on the planet. With the increased global popularity of Harley-Davidson, there are more and more motorcycle rallies cropping up worldwide. None can or will ever compare to Sturgis. It is our own history in the heartland. One of the byproducts of the attacks is that we discovered the names and faces of many of the heroic victims. Tragically, their stories were told in memoriam. In this book, we meet the everyday heroes now, and can celebrate their life and stories with them. All the characters that make our country great are found in these pages. We meet law enforcement officials, veterans, a fire fighter, and a government agent. We celebrate a sampling of the rally's great diversity: gearheads and grandmothers, newcomers and newlyweds, the young and the young at heart, the rascals and the redeemed. All brought together by a common passion for freedom.

Everybody deserves, at some time in their life, to have their story told. There were hundreds of thousands of stories floating around the Sturgis rally that week. Unfortunately, I couldn't get them all. Fortunately, I got these. Enjoy.

BABE

"This one couple that was here last year, they called us Mom and Pop. We got Christmas cards from them."

Antoinette "Babe" Pelkey has lived in the same house on Junction Street for all of her seventy-six years. She now shares her childhood home with her husband Eugene "Frank" Pelkey. Frank has only been around for fifty or so of the rallies, so he hands rally-related questions over to Babe – she has been there for all 61. Though she doesn't ride a motorcycle herself, Babe has been an active part of the rally, and can tell you how it has changed since its beginning. She tells you these stories from her shaded side lawn, where she and her husband rent out motorcycle parking in their grass for five dollars a day.

"I worked for J.C. Pennys for 43 years," Babe begins, "and during that time we would have groups of clubs come in, and they would buy towels and washcloths by the bundles – so they could polish up their bikes. On a Thursday night – it only ran then Thursday, Friday, Saturday, Sunday – they would have parades down Junction and up Main Street. Maybe this group would be all red and white, this one would be purple – and they would have clothes to match the bikes. It was great to watch them. And then, on Friday night, the Chamber of Commerce would have a free picnic for them down at the park. And they would have contests. It was fun."

> "Years ago, when I worked at the store, you didn't dare walk down Main Street."

But things changed for Babe and Sturgis in the early 1980's, when the rally took on a different atmosphere. "The gangs started to come in. The Hell's Angels and the you-know-what. They had a terrible time down at the city park. This one year they burned all the toilets and the tables…and that was the last year the park was open to the rally. The ones that used to come would be skritchy looking. Years ago, when I worked at the store, you didn't dare walk down Main Street. They'd be laying out, passed out from drugs and drinking and what not. It was a mess."

Fortunately for Babe, the rowdiness of the early 80's decreased through the 1990's. "I guess they still have the Hell's Angels, but they're not the Hell's Angels they used to be. I think they've been transformed. There's always trouble down in the campgrounds, but around here we haven't had any. Of course, you're always going to have the nudity and what not. There's always one or two that crop up."

As she tells her story, a man stops to tease her. He has parked his bike in her yard, and has purchased a few too many souvenirs on his trip into town. "Why didn't you warn me I'd need bigger saddlebags to carry all this stuff?" Babe laughs and returns the teasing. She is well-liked by those who park at her house. In some circles, she and Frank are local heroes. They've even been interviewed by the Rapid

City Journal, who wanted the rally perspective from the front porch.

Over the years, Babe and Frank have met a lot of people from all over the United States, Canada, and Australia, without ever leaving their yard. "This one couple that was here last year, they called us Mom and Pop. We got Christmas cards from them."

"What do we have during the year to offer? We have no stores."

If the rally presents any problem to the Pelkeys, it is the disastrous impact it's had on the industry in town. Businesses and houses have been torn down to make room for motorcycles. She laments the fact that the rally helps the state, but isn't always directly helpful to members of the community. "There's more vendors now then we've ever had. What do we have during the year to offer? We have no stores. The vendors have bought up all the stores on Main Street that are closed ten months of the year. When there isn't the vendors around, all you've got is concrete parking." Sadly, the J.C. Pennys store that Babe once sold bike-polishing towels from is one of many stores that has long since closed.

Even if the store was still around, Babe would have retired by now. Having that extra time at home allows her to chat more with the many visitors who pass through town. And those visits increased dramatically when she realized – accidentally – that her lawn could also be a parking lot. "A few years ago, when we were still working down at the store, we were walking in together and there's a couple bikes came in behind us. 'Excuse me, ma'am, do you live here?' 'Well, yeah.' 'I'll give you fifty dollars if we can park our bikes over here by the side of the garage.'"

A few days later, the same motorcyclists returned and paid another fifty dollars for a few hours parking. So, a tradition was born. "Everybody says, 'You're foolish not to,'" Babe explains, "What are you going to do? You can't fight'em, so you join'em. We have a ball. It's here, so accept it."

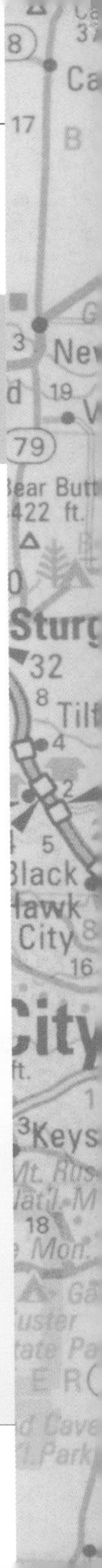

BEATRICE

"When the world sees the patch that we have on, they know that we are Christians and they can come to us."

Beatrice Roskam, 56, is a substitute teacher from Ankeny, IA. She rides as a passenger on her husband's Honda Gold Wing, and this is her fourth time at the Sturgis rally. Unlike many rally goers, Beatrice isn't here for the party or the souvenirs. She's here for the Lord.

"My husband and I are members of the Christian Motorcycle Association. We have been members since 1993. We've been Christians all of our lives. We were very active within our church, and after doing that for several years, we said 'There's more out there that we need than just church work. We need to get out and see the people of the world.' We love motorcycling, and so we got involved with Christian Motorcycle Association. We got involved because we wanted to be part of a Christian ride group. Once we got involved, we discovered that there's a ministry there. There are so many bikers who are hurting, who don't know the Lord, and they need prayer."

Beatrice and her husband go to different rallies, wearing their CMA colors, just to be a presence for anyone who needs them. They walk the streets, they help at the water wagon, they stop and minister to those who look like they need help. If it happens to be a CMA rally, their job is a little different – then they become the vendors. Beatrice explains, "Currently my husband and I are what we call 'goodie representatives' for CMA. And 'goodie representatives' means we sell shirts, and patches, and so forth for CMA, and the proceeds from that helps to keep our six evangelists on the road. So we travel the nine state region in the Midwest, and we go wherever the CMA rallies are." She's proud of the "goodies" she sells, because she knows the CMA colors are part of what makes their organization so successful. "When the world sees the patch that we have on, they know that we are Christians and they can come to us. They come to CMA members and ask that we pray for them, or whatever."

> "If they're looking for just self-gratification or whatever, they're hurting."

And what does she think about Sturgis, the biggest secular rally around? Beatrice enjoys the rally because of the different people from all over the world, and because of all the unique bikes she sees. Most of all, she likes Sturgis because it opens up her world, and provides her with new and different opportunities to minister. "Being a Christian all my life, I lived a pretty secluded life, and the things that I see I probably have never seen before, but you just know that there's people out there that are hurting, and they're looking for something. If they're looking for just self-gratification or whatever, they're hurting. You can see them. You get involved with the things of the world."

"Two years ago," Beatrice shares, "we just started our shift at the water wagon, and a girl came to me and she just gave me a big hug and she said, 'Oh, I'm so glad to see you. I just needed to tell someone that I became a Christian on the way down here.' She was a vendor. Whoever she was riding with wasn't a Christian Motorcyclist, but somebody that knew the Lord, and spoke to her about being a Christian. And she accepted the Lord. But she knew that when she got here, that she would see some of her old friends, and it was going to be a struggle. And I just hugged her and I said, 'Welcome to the Kingdom. We'll all be praying for you.' And so I went home and I asked my church people to pray for her. I've not seen her again. I have no idea if she's still walking with the Lord, but that was just good to know, because she needed to be reassured – she just needed to tell somebody that she had become a Christian."

"We plant the seed, and then they can plant the seed."

When she's not at the booth, Beatrice loves to ride and visit the local sights. She enjoys the bikes and the people and, since she and her husband wear their colors – and have CMA logos on their bike – every conversation is an opportunity to minister to someone in need, no matter who they are or where they come from. "You don't know what occupations these people have, unless you start talking to them. You walk down the street and you could be walking next to a millionaire, but you wouldn't know it. I guess that's what I find so interesting, that everybody accepts you as you are. You're a biker, and they just accept you."

"I think there probably are some people that just can't imagine how come we are doing something like this," she muses, "although I think that motorcyclists as a whole are getting a different image than they used to have. The image of motorcycling was not good in the 70's and the 80's, and I think people are looking at it differently. That's what I like to be a part of. In our own church, we're the only ones that ride a motorcycle, and when we share these experiences, they're seeing a different view. Not all are the long hair and that type of thing. There are really some neat people out there that ride a motorcycle – that love the Lord."

Of course, not everybody in Sturgis is ready for Beatrice and her message. She is sometimes concerned about the popularity of devils and skulls that show up on so much biker attire. She doesn't condemn anyone for their choices, however – she just realizes they have not yet found the answer that she has for them.

"Some are seeking. They realize we're doing a good thing, but it's always hard to tell where they are with the Lord. But there's always opportunities. A lot of them are asking about the Christian Motorcycle Association, how they can get involved – they maybe come from a state where they haven't heard about it or something…so, maybe we'll plant seeds. We plant the seed, and then they can plant the seed." All anybody needs to do, Beatrice adds, is stop by the booth and ask.

"I'm always fascinated by experiences that I hear, that CMA members have, and how they have helped someone. Just last week, Sunday, we had a testimony of a lady who was into drugs and alcohol and all this, and a CMA'er stood by her and helped her, and now she is ministering right here in Sturgis. To see someone that has been so down and so into drugs and alcoholism and so forth, and then come to know the Lord, and the change in their life, it's just….you know, God can take anybody and just change their lives. It's so encouraging."

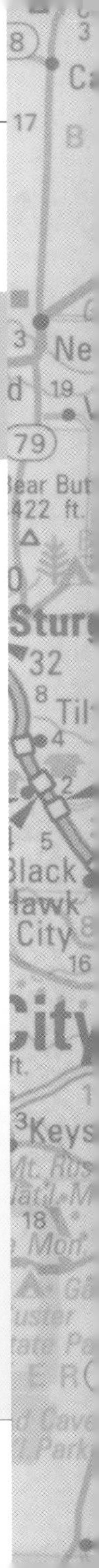

Nomad
1000

BOODAN

"I want them to like my lifestyle. I want them to live my lifestyle. Don't just stick your foot in, dive in."

He is an intimidating figure, standing there silently in the shadows. When you talk to him, you realize that Danny Ray "Boodan" Lee, 45, is also – in his own terse way - an articulate and well-spoken man. "My name's Boodan. Nomad Warlock out of Florida. Own my own tow service. My lady goes to college, she's a radiologist. I got five kids, three that are grown in the military, one in Texas, and a two-year old girl with me. Rode 2100 miles to Sturgis, and I'm having a great time, let me tell you, a really good time right now."

As a nomad, Boodan is responsible for recruiting at different rallies around the country – Laconia, Daytona, Biketoberfest – as well as smaller rallies throughout California, Texas, Kentucky, Arizona, and elsewhere. Though his main duty is recruiting, he freely admits that he comes to Sturgis mainly for the ride. "Not for the rally, for the ride. The original basic Sturgis was you'd ride your motorcycle out here. People would ride all the way across country – bikers, REAL bikers – would ride. Motorcycles all across the country come together here, party, have a great time. We all had one union thing in common, man…we LOVE to ride motorcycles. It wasn't about coming to one spot, hanging out in the bars, you know, so you'll see me or I'll see you, or we can talk. It was about US riding motorcycles. That's what I used to like about Sturgis. Now, nothing against it, there's a lot of corporate people here, a lot of Yuppies here, you know, ma and pa."

> "You know, I'll die for my patch. I'll die for my lifestyle."

Boodan has mixed feelings about the way Sturgis has changed since its earlier days. On the downside, he sees the increase in corporate bikers as similar to the white man's intrusion on the Native American population. "They're trying to enjoy my lifestyle, but they just haven't got a concept of it. It's like me, I've been to college, you wouldn't think it. But I just couldn't grasp the concept of the whole white-collar thing. You know, it's not that it's a bad thing, it just wasn't my thing. They're just sticking their toe in my lifestyle."

"There are a lot of people out here that have been riding for years and years," he adds, "they got a lot of animosity. Here these people step right out of the office, get on their

$30,000 motorcycle, and they ride down the street. They put their leather on, they have a great weekend, they raise hell, party, and then they go home…and they forget about us." The thing that he dislikes most about the increase of white-collar riders is that it has driven up the price of Harley-Davidsons. He accuses Harley of forgetting who carried them during the lean years.

On the other hand, Boodan doesn't mind the new crowd. He is, after all, a recruiter. "I want them to like my lifestyle. I want them to live my lifestyle. Don't just stick your foot in, dive in. You can still have your corporate job. You do it because you love it, not because you're trying to impress people, and that's what they're doing. They just want to impress somebody. You can't go through life like that."

"The best thing about this is these people step out of their corporate offices, the college kids come here, and they come here expecting this out of control party – violence, drugs. You know what they come here and they see? They see me walk by with my patch on, and they kind of move out of the way, but you know what? After they talk to me they kind of find out I'm just like everybody else. I'm just really extreme to what I believe in. You know, they believe in children, they'd die for their children, whatever. You know, I'll die for my patch. I'll die for my lifestyle. But that's all it is. I want them to come here and experience it because, you never know, they might start doing it all the time. If you get one in a hundred, that's one in a hundred you never had."

"This is my family. Nothing I won't do for them. It's my family."

"As long as when they look at me they don't stereotype me, 'cause I'm not going to stereotype them. They see me as living my lifestyle, and they go, 'You know what? He's not like I thought he was. He might be violent, he might be in a gang, whatever, but he's doing what he loves.' The reason you're out here putting your foot in the water is because you want to do it. Every man, EVERY MAN, every guy sitting in that college, every man at one time in his life has wanted to be a part of a gang! Every single man does. You know what? I just did it. You all had other priorities. This was mine. See, this was my family. Don't hold it against me, 'cause I'm doing what you wanted to do but just didn't."

If nothing else, the rich urban bikers can provide a source of entertainment. Boodan chuckles as he tells his favorite story from this year's rally, "The best thing downtown Sturgis I saw was a girl ride by naked – going one direction, she was headed west – and coming north and south, from both sides of the road, these guys on motorcycles were looking at her. And these were Yuppies, so it really made it even that much better for me. They ran right over each other looking at her. They were in opposite lanes and somehow they connected. And the chick, she kind of laughed, and made a right turn, and the car behind her hit the guy on the motorcycle in front of him. That was the best thing I saw. I don't want anybody to get hurt, but it was entertaining. It was free."

"Don't hold it against me, 'cause I'm doing what you wanted to do but just didn't."

But it's not all laughs for the nomadic Warlock. Boodan goes deeper into his recruiting pitch, explaining just what his patch – his colors – mean to him. "My life. My religion. Warlocks – we're a lifestyle. We believe in our brothers. There's nothing I won't do for my brother. There's nothing he won't do for me. I've been shot. I've been stabbed in my life. I've been out on the street. Thirteen years old, I was out on the street, no family. I lived in a cardboard box, ate out of Dipsy Dumpsters behind a Royal Castle hamburger... probably nobody knows what that is...it's a hamburger place. I raised myself on the street. Street gang took me in – War Lords. Got a motorcycle. Motorcycle clubs appealed to me. Just like you've got your family. There's nothing you won't do for your family. This is my family. Nothing I won't do for them. It's my family."

He explains that, while his loyalty is to the Warlocks, he is a representative for the whole lifestyle. Members of the different clubs get along – usually. He compares it to the rivalry between college football teams. While at Sturgis, Boodan is staying with members of the

Sons of Silence, and says they are treating him "like gold." Part of getting along is a necessity, because the gangs are equally under the scrutiny of the Federal Government. "All the major gangs at war with each other, we're just trying to get along 'cause, let's face it, the Feds are trying to take away our lifestyle. The Feds got a lot of power, and if you people don't pay attention to that, they'll take your rights away, too. It's not just ours, it's everybody's, whether you agree with this or not."

"I'm an ambassador-liaison. I try to promote not just my club – mostly my club, okay, I'm always plugging my club, Warlocks are like the number one club – but for all clubs. It's not like what it used to be. You got to roll with it. If you don't catch up with times they're going to roll right over the top of you. Big Brother is trying to control everything. Time to get out of the major crime rackets because, let's face it man, they're on to that. We need to get corporate. This is a business world, a business time. United States went from Stone Age to the Industrial Age. The United States now is going into the Information Age. We're going to be the information capital of the world. You better get on the ball because, if you don't, you're going to drown in the mire. And I truly believe that. That's not political, that's not me talking some good bullshit, that's the way it really, really is. You better get your ass out of the ground, you better get with it, because if you don't it's going to roll over the top of you."

"Sometimes it's a game, sometimes it's not. It's just in my lifestyle, when the game ends you're dead or you're doing life."

It's not only the Feds and the changing times that present a challenge to Boodan and his crew. In Sturgis, there's also the hassle from the local police. "Daily. Daily. Daily," he says as he slowly shakes his head. "They bang us up against the wall. They take pictures of our tattoos. They want to know where we're going, what we're doing, who we're doing it with. Everything. To protect the corporate guys. And I'm not here after the corporate guys." Boodan sniffs with disdain, but then changes his tone. "But they're

doing their job, 'cause that's how they're getting paid. Do your job, I'll do mine. They're a different gang to me, okay. I don't hate the cops. I don't like what shit they do, but let's face it, society without someone to police it is a society gone wild. I got a two-year old daughter. I don't need any Ted Bundy's out here, or Jeffrey Dahmers, so I tolerate it – it's just the way it is."

"And if you do my lifestyle," he concludes, "and you come into it, and you've got a problem with that, then don't come to my lifestyle – 'cause that's the way it is. You got to watch your P's and Q's. It's not that I mind it. Sometimes it's a game, sometimes it's not. It's just in my lifestyle, when the game ends you're dead or you're doing life."

BUELL KID

"I can understand how actors, or movie stars, or well-known people have to deal with it every day. I've just got a little touch of it."

Nick Lee still hasn't gotten used to all the attention. The 38-year-old builder/renter, performance parts promoter, and Federal semi-automatic weapons distributor from Green Bay, Wisconsin, is also gaining notoriety as a champion in the burnout pits. His skill at burnouts, or spinning his back tire until it explodes, has earned him trophies, cash, and the nicknames "The Burnout King" or the "Buell Kid" in his short three-year career.

Nick explains how it all began. "In '98, the first year I came on my purple nitrous bike, I went to Sundance, Wyoming to the burnout contest. It's a neat little town. My buddy said, 'Hey, man, you got to enter this.' I said all right. I ended up being one of the last guys to go, and everybody was just doing their normal sitting-in-one-spot burnouts, and I started doing donuts. Because it's nitrous oxide, when I hit the nitrous the pipe gets really hot and my pants started on fire, and I didn't know that. When I got done, my buddy was putting out my pants and the crowd – I was really shocked – the crowd, they were throwing beer cans and they rushed in and, all of a sudden, you're in the spotlight. I had so much attention focused on me. It's kind of like a stardom thing. These people were just overwhelmed with what I did, and it's just, you know, like 'Hey, that was the greatest thing.' I couldn't believe it. It's like winning a Superbowl or something. People say, 'We've never seen it like that.' 'You made my vacation.' 'That was the coolest thing.' 'We didn't know a Buell could do this.' They just love seeing that stuff. I have a little bit of a problem with the attention thing. I'm not used to that. I can understand how actors, or movie stars, or well-known people have to deal with it every day. I've just got a little touch of it."

Nick likes it, however, when the crowd comments on his motorcycle – a 2001 Buell. He's proud of the fact that his sports bike is made by Harley, and is not "a rice grinder," as some folks refer to the Japanese sport bikes. He's trying to catch Harley-Davidson's eye at these competitions, and would like to work out some type of endorsement or a burnout tour. While he has the ability to build his own bikes, his goal is to help put "Buell on the map."

"Building the bikes is a hobby," he explains. "I was thinking of doing it as a living, but there's a lot of competition. I'm too picky and meticulous with my things, so I might build one or two really high end dollar bikes a year, or for a customer who wants just one person to work on it."

Though he spends most of his time on the "high end dollar" bikes, Nick enjoys the variety of all the bikes he sees on the streets of Sturgis, including one he saw made out of an outhouse. He has no problem with the cross section of income at the rally, and sees a place for both the common everyday rider and the Rich Urban Biker. "Lawyers, doctors, anybody in the professions, everybody has to stay somewhere. That's where the backbone of your money is coming in. Those people are the ones that bring in the huge dollars. Some of these bikes here are $75-100 thousand dollars. I think it's pretty neat, because everybody wants their own paint, their own unique thing. There's nothing wrong with that."

"Every year I come out here I learn something different. Every Year."

"I don't think anybody will put you down for riding anything here. If you got wheels, you know... Some people can't afford a lot of these high dollar bikes. People just want to be part of driving around, looking around, seeing things."

And "seeing things" is one of Nick's favorite activities. When he's not in a competition, he likes to enjoy all that Sturgis has to offer. "The people. The food. Man, I love the food, 'cause I can't cook shit. The weather, I love the hot weather. Looking at different product for bikes, 'cause I am building a couple of custom bikes myself. The scenery. Definitely the scenery. Driving around the mountains and that is definitely unbelievable. This year for the first time I went out to Mt. Rushmore to see the heads – the president heads. Those roads can get pretty hairy. One screw up and you're done. You're off a cliff."

"I do see a lot of sport bikes here," Nick adds, comparing the type of bike he rides to the traditional cruiser or street bike that dominates much of the rally. "Not as much as Daytona. They got a whole sport, crotch rocket is what they call them, section. I see more of a problem at Daytona with the sport bikes. A lot of go-getters. Magazine racers, is what I call'em. I've been to Daytona, Myrtle Beach,

Laughlin…Sturgis is definitely the hugest rally. No doubt. It just brings people from all over the country."

"I look forward to driving out here every year. I meet new friends every year. Fantastic people. It's getting to be like a family, a home away from home. Every year I come out here I learn something different. Every year."

"It's a good experience, I'd recommend to anybody, even if you don't have a bike." And who knows? If you don't have a bike, maybe Nick will give you a ride, as he did to some children he met in Deadwood. "A grandma and a grandpa came up, they had two grandkids. We said, 'Hey, let's throw them on here, take them for a ride.' They said, 'Why would you do that? Take your time to ride with them?' I was their highlight. We got pictures and stuff. We rode'em around the block. They'd never been on a Harley. They were just so thankful about it."

Perhaps it's gestures like that which draw people to the Buell Kid. If that's the case, Nick will have to get accustomed to the attention, and stories like this one that he shares. "I had a guy a couple of years ago come up driving a mid-70's AMF Harley. I mean, the thing was leaking oil…this thing was just a pile of…just a pile, put it that way. I try to talk to everybody…to try to be as nice as possible. The guy's pulling out a couple of dollars to give me money for a new tire. The guy's like, 'You know, I work all year. This is the only thing I got going in my life. That was the greatest thing I ever saw. You just made my vacation.' I didn't want to take his money, but he was like 'No, no,' and I thought, well I better take it to make him feel good. The guy needed the money to put the oil in the oil tank for his bike. When people start coming up and saying things like that, it sticks in your mind. A lot of people have a lot of respect for me, I really didn't realize, and it's getting bigger and bigger."

"Those roads can get pretty hairy. One screw up and you're done. You're off a cliff."

Thinking about that and other stories, Nick shudders slightly, "I can't image the people with pictures of me around this country. It's really weird."

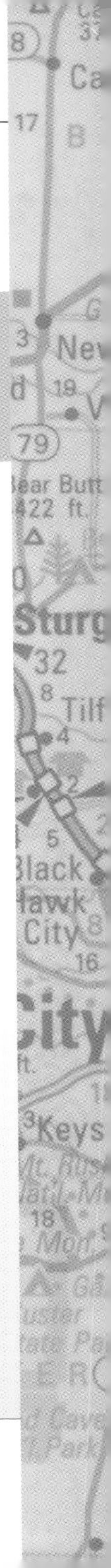

CHARLIE

*"I'm in a war zone compared to this place.
This is heaven. This is the only show on earth."*

He is a giant man, towering over anyone and anything around him, including the white 1998 Harley-Davidson FHTCU that he calls "Baby." Sergeant Charles Redstone, Jr., who goes by Charlie, is a 54-year-old police officer from Hackensack, New Jersey. He is also, as the Nam Knights patch on the back of his vest tells you, a veteran. "I'm with a group of motorcyclists; we're Viet Nam veterans. Most of us are Viet Nam veterans and police officers. I'm out of the New Jersey chapter."

The war is a topic that Charlie feels strongly about. "I was in the service from '66 to '69. I did my time in Nam in '67. It wasn't bad, because I only did six months over there. I got wounded and so I got out early. I lost probably a third of my graduating high school class of '66. We could have been there in a much stronger capacity and done what we should have. We should have gone in and kicked ass, and then come out. We wouldn't have lost as many guys."

"There's a lot of guys over there," Charlie huffs, "whether they're in the ground or they're walking dead, they're there, and they should be home where they belong – in the cemetery of their town or their state, with their loved ones. This country sold us down the river – politics. Instead of being hard and saying, 'Listen, we want the bodies out of there, we want our men back, we want an accounting of the men that were there,' we didn't Our men pussy-footed around. Some of our senators who were there as prisoners of war are pussyfooting around. They're not doing what they should. If they are, they're sure not vocal enough that I can hear them. And I'm one of the guys that was there, and it's not right."

Ironically, the injustice doesn't seem to end there. Here we have a U.S. veteran, wounded in action, still carrying the weight of his lost brethren on his huge shoulders. If that's not enough, we also learn that police officer Charlie has been wounded in the line of duty. "I got hit by a drunk driver five years ago, and I had to get back surgery, and they fused three disks. I had a fight with a drug dealer last year, and he worked on the forth disk" Adding insult to injury, the latest damage will probably end Charlie's career as a motorcyclist. "Looks like I'm going to be going for back surgery, so this is probably going to be my last ride. When I get home I'm selling my ride, and looking to retire in April of next year. So we're getting rid of Baby, and I'll go for surgery, and then I'm moving down to Florida for the heat."

At that Charlie stops and bellows. "I'm saying to myself, 'Heat? I'll just come to South Dakota for the heat." Right now, it's approximately 115 degrees. After hearing about South Dakota winters, which can easily reach 50 below, Charlie goes back to his original plan. "We're staying in Florida."

Still, Charlie and his wife, who rode with him from New Jersey, are very impressed with South Dakota. "This is our first trip out here and I'm telling you I love it. I love it! This takes my breath away. This is God's country. From where we're at, in Jersey, you wouldn't believe what I see. I'm in a war zone compared to this place. This is heaven. This is the only show on earth." As he praises the scenery, Charlie's tone shifts slightly from poetic to political. "I'm riding down 90 and I'm looking at hills, and I'm saying to myself, 'Imagine the buffalo that came over these hills.' I'm part Cheyenne, and I got a lot of respect for the American Indian. Unfortunately, our government never had as much respect, they broke every treaty. But this is their country, this is their land. It's beautiful."

"I'm part Cheyenne, and I got a lot of respect for the American Indian."

Conversation turns to the Sturgis rally itself, and what brought the Redstones out here. "This is the granddaddy. This is the big boy. My wife and I, we had to make this trip. We'll probably never get to do this again. My wife and I have a thing where, when we're old and gray living together, we're not going to say 'We wish we'd have done that' or 'We should have done that.' We're going to say, 'Honey, remember 2001 when we drove eighteen hundred miles to go to Sturgis?' So that's it, that's why we wanted to be here."

Fortunately for Charlie, he not only made it out here, he had a place to stay when he arrived. "We got lucky. The word was, you're never going to find a room. I'm on AOL, and I run a WAV list, where I send out old music Monday to Friday, five songs a day, fifties and sixties music. This young lady was on my list, and she says, 'Oh, you're going to Sturgis? My next door neighbor's daughter lives in Spearfish. We might be able to get you a room.' I'm looking around, there's guys, they're living in tents in this place. I'm saying, 'A room!'

By the grace of God we got lucky."

Funny enough, a lot of people on this planet wouldn't view just "a room" as either luck or the grace of God. But not everybody has the no-nonsense philosophy of Charlie Redstone. For example, Charlie says, "We're all entitled to move up in the world. If you have the means, the wherewithal, that you want to do something different, that you want to move to someplace.... I'm born and raised in New Jersey, and I don't want to die there. We got fifty states in this goddamn country, this is a beautiful country, and we go wherever we want to go. And it doesn't matter what our status is, what our color is." Pointing to the hills around him, Charlie continues with his platform. "I say God bless anybody who wants to make a move out to a country like this. I can't find fault with anybody who wants to make this kind of a move because they want to get in touch with nature, maybe, or they want to get away from the congestion, or they want to spend their last few years in peace, quiet, and harmony with the land, instead of being closed in by a group of people. I wouldn't mind living out here at all...except it's hot!"

"I say God bless anybody who wants to make a move out to a country like this."

In spite of the heat, Charlie has accomplished all that he needs to. "Been to town twice. Got my bike taken care of...We picked up our t-shirts and our hats for the people that didn't make it. I'm glad that we were able to make this. We met some beautiful people out here, very hospitable, very polite, very entertaining. I loved it. It's a great state."

Charlie pauses, and thinks for a moment about this, his large brow furrowing. This is his last great ride across America. "Tomorrow morning we're leaving. We're not going to come back." It would be a sad thought, if giant Charlie weren't ready with a shrug and a punch line. "Eighteen hundred miles for a t-shirt."

Amoco
WELCOME RIDERS!
Lite
Welcome to
STURGIS
HONDA
CBR
600F3

CHRIS

"Basically, I don't fit in at all. But, I don't know, I like to ride, so I take part in it."

The first thing you think when you see 19-year-old Chris Roberts riding down the street is "What is HE doing here?" Clean cut and clean shaven, and no leather clothing anywhere, this freshman at the South Dakota School of Mines and Technology in Rapid City does not look like your typical Sturgis goer. To top it off, he rides a 1995 Honda CBR 600. So you have to ask, "What are doing out here on a Japanese sport bike?"

"Basically, I don't fit in at all," Chris explains with a smile, "But, I don't know, I like to ride, so I take part in it."

"It's just the age, I guess. But definitely someday I want a Harley for sure."

Does anybody give him a bad time about the bike? "Not personally, but I had some friends in the same situation that did. Just verbal abuse, I guess. Things like 'Get a real bike,' along those lines. I think it was pretty much all kind of teasing. It's just because of the fact there's mostly Harleys around. We're just part of the minority group this week."

What he rides also explains what he wears. Chris sticks with jeans, tennis shoes, and plain t-shirts. "Basically, the look goes with the bike. If I was on a Harley, I'd be in leather, and black, and boots, and all that." Someday, when finances allow, he plans to join the whole look, bike and all, but for now it's the sport bike. Of course, the sport bike fits not only his income, but also his image. "It's just the age, I guess. But definitely someday I want a Harley for sure."

Whatever he rides, Chris is a bit of an expert on the rally. Born and raised just down the road in Deadwood, he has been to the rally every year since he was twelve. He still enjoys it. "Pretty much a good time. See a lot of people, a lot of new faces. You experience something new every time you go." He's been to Daytona and thinks that, by comparison, Sturgis is special – mostly because of the scenery and local attractions. "I think a lot of it has to do with the area that they come to, and what goes on here for the bikers. There's a little something for everybody here. You might have to know where to look a little bit, but everybody can find something that they'll enjoy."

Of course, being from the area, Chris has visited all the sights, so his "attractions" are a little different. "I pretty much just like to people watch. The rally's in my home area so there's nothing for me to go see that I already haven't seen, so I just pretty much watch the people who come in." As he's watched the people over the years, he's noticed some changes in the way they behave, and the way outsiders view them. "It's a little less rowdy, maybe. People look at bikers different, I think. I know I do. Being a little kid, I used to look at them as – I don't know – maybe the scary type. But now they're the nice guys, the good guys."

Chris recognizes that the increase in biker "good guys" is probably because there are more corporate types in the crowd than ever before. "I don't have a problem with it. I personally know quite a few people who the other fifty-one weeks out of the year are behind a desk, and in their suit…and they decide to come out for Bike Week, and get in leather, and take their bike out for one week. That's just their thing, that's just their way of getting away from it all and having fun." And even if they ride for only one week a year, Chris doesn't feel that this damages the integrity of the motorcycling culture. "I can't really see a reason that it would hurt it at all. It'd only be an image that it would be hurting. I don't see that that is a big deal."

"All my peers and friends love going to Sturgis."

Despite having lived in the area all his life, Chris has only been riding for about four months. In this short time, it is a hobby that his peer group quickly accepted. "They all think that motorcycling is cool, and those that aren't involved want to be. All my peers and friends love going to Sturgis. It's a lot of a mutual thing. There's no disagreements with me doing what I do."

Though his peers may be on his side, not all rally goers are pleased with the small but noticeable sport bike population. Many are concerned that the young riders on these faster, lighter bikes are dangerous to have around. "I probably agree with them, that it can be unsafe. I try to be good when I'm around a lot of traffic and things like that. I never take off and do my thing when there's a lot of people around, or anybody else that could be hurt by a mistake that I would make. But I see a lot of people that are stupid around heavy traffic areas. People have a reason to worry about it."

But when he's out in open, does he crank it up? "Sometimes, yeah," Chris replies with a sly grin, "If the conditions are right."

NOT ILLEGAL
ROYAL

DENNIS

"I'd hate to see motorcycling die as an entertainment, because it is one of the best entertainments you can go with."

"Sturgis is one of my main rallies a year. I worked construction up until last year, and so lot of times I'm close enough to Sturgis so I could ride up, and I'll usually spend three or four days out here." Such was the life of Dennis Monahan, as he adjusted his work schedule to make room for a total of thirty-five Sturgis rallies. This year is different. Now that he's out of the construction game, the 60-year-old rally regular is working for the first time as a vendor, selling goods at the Crazy Horse Trading Company just outside the Sturgis city limits. "Oh, yeah, it's a lot different. You can't get out and run around like you do if you're a tourist up here. We came up a week and a half early and got all of our riding in. We rode about a thousand miles through the Black Hills, went out to Rushmore, out to Spearfish Canyon, to Custer, to Devil's Tower in Wyoming…all around."

"This is a new place for us," says Dennis, referring to the Crazy Horse tent. "We were in Sturgis for ten years, and we decided this year, we want to kind of relax and enjoy ourselves but make a little money, too. We don't make as much money out here, but we'll cover our expenses and stuff like that." While working the booth may cut into some of Dennis' riding time, it certainly increases the number of rallies he gets to attend. "Now that I'm vending and stuff, we go to 25-30 rallies a year, and before that, I'd probably make five, six, seven rallies a year, and probably four or five bike shows."

"I don't go to a rally to trailer my bike, I ride."

When he compares the rallies, Dennis observes that they all have one thing in common – it's all about money. "The only thing that I don't care about most of these rallies and stuff nowadays, it's just becoming too damn commercial. Everybody trying to make a buck. You got to support it, and stuff like that, but some of the stuff – some of the prices - is getting a little outrageous." Sturgis is just as guilty as the others, he adds, especially paying for vending space and lodging within the city limits. "It's awful expensive to come to Sturgis, even as a bike rider, because it just costs you so much. They raise the prices on the goods and stuff down here, and if you get a motel it's twice of what it normally is. I do like the old rallies and stuff when you'd rough it and that was it. You went out there to find you a place to have a good meeting and rough it. There's a lot of rallies we go to that we pretty well nothing but rough it. Some of the newer generation will come down, and they'll rent motel rooms, but a majority of the old bikers, if they go to a small rally – a two or three day rally – they rough it. When you first came here, there were very few campgrounds, places where you could really find a good place with facilities and stuff." Now there are plenty of hotels and full facility campgrounds to stay in around Sturgis.

"The old bikers were the chosen few, you know."

That change, Dennis explains, is due to the increase in motorcyclists on the road, mostly the newer generation of professionals who ride bikes. "Thirty-five years ago, when you first come to Sturgis, there's probably three or four thousand people. They're estimating 350,000 this year, and that's by what's already came in already. You got more people than ever riding bikes now, and the new generation, that's a little bit different type of biker than the old bikers. The old bikers were the chosen few, you know. Most people didn't know that you could get out and ride a motorcycle, that you could actually be safe on one. Most people were scared of them. Now, more and more people know that you can ride a bike and do it safely."

Even though Dennis is sometimes amused by the young professionals who purchase Crazy Horse's latest product – a cushion for a motorcycle's shift peg which keeps the peg from scuffing the rider's shoes – he is not bothered by the changes they bring to the motorcycling landscape. "It don't make any difference. It's changing with the times. I can't say there's anything really bad about how it's turning out – the new generation and stuff like that. I like to see people enjoy themselves, and that's one good way to enjoy yourself. Biking's becoming more of a family thing these nowadays, too, and I like to see that. A lot more women are riding their own bikes today, where before, traditionally, a woman did not ride her own bike." All of these are good things, Dennis argues, because it keeps the sport alive. "I'd hate to see motorcycling die as an entertainment, because it is one of the best entertainments you can go with. It's not any more dangerous than scuba diving or anything else. I like to see people get out and ride."

With the increase in professionals, families, and women, Dennis observes that the Sturgis rally – despite the large numbers – is actually rather tame. In fact, compared to other rallies he attends, Sturgis is actually stricter with its rules and law enforcement than elsewhere. Of course, those restrictions would never stop Dennis from good, clean fun. He shakes his head and laughs softly as he explains that he's never gotten too out of hand. "Not outside the usual parties and stuff like that. Like one time we took a little gal named Shadow and, she got pretty well drunk and she went to bed. The next morning she got up and she really had a hangover, and we took and taped her in the porta potty. She was cussing' us and telling us she was going to kill us all when she got out of there. Things like that."

So, other than the occasional prank, the rally seems a pretty safe place. "The only problem I've seen," says Dennis, "is with some of the younger breed coming to a rally, and I haven't seen it so much here. They get out and get wild on their bikes; they get a little drunk, get a little stupid. But other than that, no, I don't see any problem." Speaking of this younger, wilder breed, Dennis also has his opinions on the sport bikes that they ride. "I just don't care for them. They were originally made to be a racing bike, and as far as I'm concerned, that's what they are. I can't see bending over the handlebars and laying down, and riding for a couple of hundred miles. It's the most uncomfortable thing I've ever seen."

And, after so many years of coming to the rally, Dennis knows a thing or two about riding. Unfortunately, this year – because of the vending booth – he had to trailer his bike. "I don't go to a rally to trailer my bike, I ride. Driving up here was kind of boring to me, 'cause I'm used to riding. I'd rather ride than drive anyway, so that's just it. I've been riding ever since I was a little kid. Back when my kids were home, my wife drove the car and I rode." But trailering is just one of the trade-offs that goes with the territory.

The other trade-off in Dennis' life is that, despite his love for Harley-Davidsons, he rides a Honda Gold Wing. "Most of your other bikes are accepted today, because they are big bikes and everything. The reason I ride a Gold Wing is several years ago I broke my back and I couldn't take the 'Harley shakes' for a while. For about four and a half years, I couldn't ride, and then when I could, I'd ride that old Knucklehead of mine for fifty miles, and I'd have to go in for therapy." Dennis pauses, then points out that Harley-Davidson is now making smoother riding machines. Then, with a dreamy look in his eyes, he concludes, "In fact, I'm gonna order me a new Electra Glide."

THROTTLE SALOON
JACK

Doug & Diane

"We have the same moral background. The same values. We love Harleys. We're really happy, positive folks."

It was a match made in Harley heaven. Doug, age 44, met 35-year-old Diane – whom people call "The Road Queen" - at their local Harley-Davidson dealership back in St. George, Utah. He rides a 1983 Harley FLH Fatboy, and she rides a 2000 Road King (er, make that Queen). They started riding together with a small club from the dealership, and the rest, as they say, is history. "Lots of rallies, and parties," says Diane, "and we fell in love."

This is their wedding day. They are the first couple to be married at The Full Throttle Saloon in Sturgis, the largest biker bar in the world. "Our motto is 'Live Life Full Throttle,'" Diane explains, speaking loudly to be heard over the blare of rock'n'roll reception music in the background, "and we made a pact before we even began dating that if we got a tattoo, too, it was going to say 'Live Life Full Throttle' – because that's Evel Knievel's tattoo. So, the president of our club, who's here with us today, says 'You know, there's a Full Throttle Saloon in Sturgis.' Where else could we get married?"

"And the best thing," Doug adds, "is we started out friends before anything else. I always considered her a high maintenance girlfriend, so I wanted to stay away from her, as far as getting hooked. I wanted to be a friend and ride with her and stuff, 'cause she's really fun to follow on her big Road Queen. One day she calls me up – she's got a fancy boyfriend down there in California that she was going to go visit – she calls me on the phone and says 'I need to talk to you.' Okay, I go over there to her house to visit, she tells me 'I think I'm falling in love with you.' I says 'You just go visit your boyfriend down in California. I'll be here waiting for you if you want to come home. If not, if you want to stay down there, that's groovy.' And so she was down there, and staying in some fancy hotel. And I called up there and the guy goes, 'Oh, these are restricted rooms.' I said, 'Brother, there's a fifty dollar tip in it for you – you do the champagne, and the flowers, and the chocolate covered strawberries.' He said, 'Mr. Griffiths, everything is done for you,' and I go 'Right on, bro.' She got the champagne…she come back from that deal…." Diane finishes the story, "I came home to him."

Once they decided to get married, it was time to make the arrangements. The first step was checking with the Full Throttle Saloon. "We contacted them over the Internet," says Doug, "The lady called us back – the owner of the place – and said she would be honored if we were here. And for their first marriage, they're going to put us on their website." Once the locale was set up, Doug continues, they needed to find someone to perform the ceremony. "We contacted the CMA motorcycle association. They had one of their members come over and marry us. He was a preacher." Then, just as you would expect to find with married couples, Doug and Diane complete the preacher story in a rapid fire tag-team of words.

Diane: "They were so generous and kind. They were great."

Doug: "It's just been really nice, and we're really proud to say the CMA motorcycle association married us. We wanted someone a little off the wall. We asked for the biggest, dirtiest, biker-looking guy they had."

Diane: "He kind of looked like Colonel Sanders."

Doug: "He was a really great guy. Great people. And they were married how many years?"

Diane: "Thirty-nine. So they gave us some good advice."

Doug: "Good advice on what we need to do to stay married and everything."

The rapid fire dialogue continues as Doug and Diane share more about their wedding arrangements, including the interesting reactions from family members – most of whom belong to the church of Latter Day Saints.

Doug: "We brought her grandparents from St. George, Utah…"

Diane: "…and my mom, and the dog…"

Doug: "…and her grandparents are staunch LDS people. This is a very big eye opener for them. They're about seventy-five years old…"

Diane laughs and screams: "Naked people!"

Doug: "There's people riding naked through the campground. I think that's the first time the grandmother ever seen another man naked besides her husband…and she did say the man had a nice belly."

The next decision to be made was the wedding attire. White gowns and tuxes didn't seem quite right. They decided to go with Diane's favorite motif – flames. "She loves flames," Doug explains, "Bikes need flames. We looked for flames on everything we were doing." Diane adds, "We have a flame club at home, a little group of us, who wear nothing but flames. I wear flame underwear with my chaps. It's good." Fortunately, they found some nice black shirts with red and yellow flames for Doug and for members of the wedding party. "Like her grandparents," Doug smiles, "they come to the thing, put on flame shirts, black glasses…they've just been great sported all the way with this."

Everything was set. They had a place, a preacher, plenty of relatives and invited guests…even a flame theme to pull it all together. The only possible snag was that Diane had to get Doug out of the Sturgis jail in time to get to the ceremony. "They put him in jail," Diane exclaims, "I had to go bail him out so I could marry him." Doug begins to explain his mishaps with local law enforcement since they arrived in Sturgis. "We first pull in to town…it was 10 o'clock at night…so I put my goggles up on my face…" Diane interjects, "We rode 450 miles that day – covered in bugs." "So I couldn't see," Doug continues, "so I pull up my goggles. Not two minutes later a police officer pulls me over and tells me you have to wear eye protection. And he starts checking the bike and everything, so that's okay. So the next night we're out, goofing around and stuff, and we're out to the Broken Spoke Saloon. I was going to pick up my girlfriend – at that time – and I make a U turn. Officer pulls me over, says 'Have you been drinking?' I go, 'Well, I just left the Broken Spoke. We've been drinking all day long, sort of here and there, checking out the venues and stuff. Gives me the Breathalyzer. South Dakota law is 1.0, I pull a 1.3. So they take me to jail. I tell the police, 'I'm getting married on Tuesday!'" Diane chips in at this point, "Yeah, me and mom were there to bail him out. Grandma doesn't want to leave the campground. She's afraid she'll get arrested if she goes anywhere. Grandma's mortified. She doesn't want to go to jail." Once out of jail, the wedding took place without a hitch. The only crimp the DUI charge put into the wedding schedule was it eliminated their plans to do a burnout on the Harley right after the ceremony as the happy couple took off from the parking lot.

"Bikes need flames. We looked for flames on everything we were doing."

Unfortunately, South Dakota law says that Doug cannot ride his bike in the state, and has to trailer it across the state line before he can take it on the roads again.

Of course, that little restriction won't stop them from participating in the evening motorcycle parade held nightly at their campground; a parade well known for the little to no clothing worn by some of the riders. Diane elaborates with a grin, "And I'm wearing the coolest underwear you've ever seen. I got on the good stuff…really, really good stuff. We're going to out for a little spin tonight in the campgrounds. Have ourselves a yee-ha." Knowing that this interview might someday show up in book form, Diane thinks of a way to help re-live the "yee-ha" ride, "Maybe I'll show up in my underwear and sign autographs."

Clearly, these two suit each other very well. They seem to agree on most issues, until the topic of wealthy urban bikers comes up.

Diane: "I love Yuppies."

Doug: "Yuppies suck."

Diane: "I am a Yuppie."

The disagreement is short-lived, however, as Doug concedes that "the good thing is, if you ride, you ride. No matter what, if you've have something good between your legs, then you're having a great time." Diane builds on his statement, adding, "Your social status does not affect who you are that way. All of us love the wind. Love the smell of burning rubber. That goes across all social barriers, and we are all one together." Doug agrees with Diane, and admits that his negative view of yuppies was influenced by the way he thought, and was treated, in his younger motorcycling years. "I've been into motorcycles since I was a young kid," he says, "In the days, when you rode Harleys, you were looked at pretty hard. I've had truck drivers ride me off the road. I've had people shoot at me. I've had people try to fight with me because I was on a motorcycle. It's not like back in the old days, when it's more of an outlaw thing. I never got involved with drugs and that outlaw stuff, but I've had friends and people I know very near to me that aren't around today because of those experiences they're involved with. They ought to be with their families, but they're locked away in prison. The motorcycling thing's come a long way since then. Nowadays…what I really like to see is different people get involved in the motorcycle world. It's been really good for motorcycles, especially Harleys." Diane nods, then makes a face and adds, "And it sent the price right through the roof. I spent $27,000 on my bike."

More important than whether or not they agree on yuppie bikers, Doug and Diane seem to agree on basic philosophies of life and family. Doug is quick to point out one of the reasons he is so in love with Diane. "You know, I'm 44 years old. I've been commonly law married. I have a seventeen-year-old daughter that I've had custody of since she was two years old. And Diane's taken her right in as a mother. My daughter don't know her mother very well; she's never been part of her life. And Diane's taken that position very well. Everything just seemed to click really good." Catching up on his serious tone, Diane reveals a more somber perspective on their relationship, "When we die, we want to be out there together on the bikes. That's what we want. My dad just died of cancer a week ago Friday – a horrible way, brain cancer. And, you know, people give me shit about the Harley, and the helmet, and all that mess. I don't wear a helmet on purpose. If I get hit, I want to be gone."

Doug explains that these connections stem from their common beliefs. "We're both LDS, you know – from Utah – the way we were brought up and stuff." Diane reaches over and grabs his hand. "We have the same moral background," she adds, "The same values. We love Harleys. We're really happy, positive folks." And do the LDS folks back home get it? Diane thinks, nods slightly, and says, "The ones that do are the happiest."

The conversation finally turns to Sturgis itself. This is Doug's second trip; he was here in 1986. This is Diane's first time, and she thinks it's fabulous. "Extra, extra motorcycles. Extra, extra leather. Oh, yeah." Doug, too, has no complaints. "It's been a great time. I can't blame the police officers for doing the stuff. They're out there doing their job. I did something I shouldn't. I shouldn't have made that U turn. I seen other people do it, so I thought it was cool, but it wasn't." He continues, "It's really fun to see people get together like this. Since we got married here in the Full Throttle, we've had people we don't even know taking pictures, offer us congratulations, giving us money. And we don't know any of these people. And that's what the motorcycling thing is all about; people getting together and having a great time."

Diane nods and adds, "Camaraderie."

"It's been really fun for us," exclaims Doug, "We're just really happy we've been able to come out here and do this. I get a DUI, I get thrown in jail, I get out, I get married. My whole life is totally changed."

"So," Diane says, summing it all up, "it's the perfect Harley-Davidson romance."

EDDY K

"We tease each other all the time, but the truth of the matter is – you cannot beat the ride across country on a Gold Wing."

"I'm from Maryland, just outside of Washington DC," says Special Agent Edward "Eddy K" Kerrick, Sr. "I work for the government, for the United States Department of Congress. I do primarily protection for the Secretary of Commerce."

Eddy K has a serious job. It's no wonder that he rides a serious motorcycle, and for seriously long distances. To get to Sturgis, the 45-year-old government agent traveled from one end of the country to the other on his 1992 Honda Gold Wing. He rides with an African-American motorcycle club, all of whom are on big-engine touring bikes. "This group is Independent C.C. Riders Motorcycle Club, out of southern Maryland, Pennsylvania, and Delaware. And basically we're a group of guys, love riding motorcycles, having a good time, you know. We do a lot of charity stuff back in our area. C.C. actually stands for Charles County, which is where the original home of the group is."

"We came out here with thirteen. Some of them broke off, so we got about eight of us left." Eddy points to a few of his club members who are wandering the vendor booths across the street from where their bikes are parked. "We came out and went to Las Vegas, we left Las Vegas and went to a rally in Fresno, California, and from Fresno we did some sightseeing in San Francisco and stuff. We left Fresno on Monday and started on our way here."

"It's quite an experience. I've never seen anything of quite this magnitude."

This is Eddy's first time at Sturgis. "It's huge! It's quite an experience. I've never seen anything of quite this magnitude. I've been to Americade several years, and I thought that was huge, but this by far takes it." His reason for coming to Sturgis he can sum up in one word. "Curiosity. I hear so much about it, I basically wanted to see it for myself." While he's here, he plans to do just what he's been doing all across the country – riding and looking. "We're doing some sightseeing. We're going to see Mt. Rushmore, the Crazy Horse memorial, and just take in as much as we can in a couple of days, and head back east."

Having been to so many other rallies and locations, Eddy can speak with authority on some of the things that makes Sturgis different. Those things might not always be in his favor. For example, Sturgis is dominated by Harley-Davidson, and he's riding a Honda. "We got one Harley riding with us, actually. We had a couple more before they broke off. We tease each other all the time, but the truth of the matter is – you cannot beat the ride across country on a Gold Wing. It's just a smooth ride. I mean, I love Harleys, don't get me wrong, I plan on owning one – but I also will keep this Gold Wing. For the overall smoothness and comfort, it's hard to beat. We do a lot of touring, and that's primarily why we ride Gold Wings."

"Sturgis is a predominantly white event. In fact, I don't think I've seen, besides my group, but one other African-American thus far."

Not only are there a lot of Harleys at Sturgis, there are also a lot of Caucasians. You can't help but notice that motorcycling, especially in the upper Midwest, is an activity without a lot of racial diversity. "Sturgis is a predominantly white event," Eddy agrees. "In fact, I don't think I've seen, besides my group, but one other African-American thus far. I'm sure there's probably some more here, but it's a predominantly white event. Americade is pretty well mixed; it's still predominantly white. The event we went to in Fresno, which was black bikers – it's not dubbed the black bikers – but it is, you know – but it was a good mixture of both white and black." As for Sturgis, Eddy understands that the lack of diversity is nothing purposeful; it's just the way it is. "It doesn't bother me, personally, I just love motorcycling – and motorcycle events and motorcycle people. Everybody I've met so far has been pretty friendly. I haven't met any bad people yet. I haven't had a bad time. I haven't encountered any racial overtones. It's been nice."

Eddy knows that, not only is the racial mixture in motorcycling becoming more diverse, the social class mixture is evolving as well. "A lot of the people I ride with are professionals. I'm also a member of the Maryland chapter of the

Blue Knights, which is predominantly law enforcement officers. It's being taken over; it's going first class. I think it's wonderful. It actually enriches the social climate of motorcycling, because you don't have just these wanna-be bad guys, so to speak. You've got real people that do real jobs in the real world, and they're just realizing the excitement and fun that revolves around motorcycling. It's a good thing."

"We encountered in our travels a few Hell's Angels, and they were really nice guys."

He occasionally encounters the hardcore side of the biker culture, but – as both a rider and as a government agent – he has never had any trouble. "The bike rally we were at out in Fresno, they had the outlaw clubs out there, supposedly the really bad guys, but they behaved themselves. The law enforcement agencies in all these towns are just not tolerating it anymore. They're bringing in extra help and they're keeping it controlled now." In fact, Eddy grins, sometimes those lines even overlap. "We encountered in our travels a few Hell's Angels, and they were really nice guys. One of them went as far as to explain that he was actually a doctor, and that they were working very hard to change the image of the Hell's Angels. It's coming around."

All races. All classes. This is the America that Eddy K works for, and this trip has made those lessons all the more valuable. "I've had a wonderful time. You know, you hear so many people talking about wanting to go overseas, and I've been overseas to see different things on vacation, but until this cross-country trip, I did not realize how beautiful this country that we have is. There's a lot to see. It has only stirred my curiosity to even see more of it. This is a beautiful country we have."

GENUINE

HERB

"I've had some good experiences and I've had some bad. I can't say that I've ever come out here and gone home disappointed yet."

Herb Heidecker, age 51, from Glencoe, MN, has been a regular fixture on the Sturgis main street for the past fifteen years. "I'm a people watcher, especially the girls," Herb says, in a soft and slightly hoarse voice, "I like to spend a lot of time down here. I could come here and just sit all day downtown, just taking pictures and watching people, 'cause I enjoy it." When he's not watching the girlish figures in Sturgis, the semi-retired business owner is watching statistical figures back home. "I own an information service for lawyers and chiropractors. I collect accident and criminal data. I give it to them, and they in turn mail it off for solicitation of business. I've been in the business for seven years. I am probably the biggest competitor in the Twin Cities, Minnesota, and I supply even to other competitors. Basically, I'm retired, but I still own the business."

Given Herb's skills at information gathering, and his long history at the rally, he is an expert on the changes that have taken place over the years. "I seen it go somewhat family orientated. The vendors have grown in numbers. The people have grown in numbers. It's gotten real congested at times, with the traffic. On the fiftieth, it took forty-five minutes to get out of town. That was a real bad one that year. But it don't bother me. I don't mind traffic 'cause I put up with it every day for seven years driving the freeways of Minneapolis-St. Paul."

"This place is well loved all over the world."

Despite the congestion, Herb likes the increased focus on families. "I think it's for the better. There's a lot of little, younger, nine or so and up – that enjoy it out here. Just to see what the bikers are all about...what the rally is all about...the races. I had my daughter out here, she was thirteen or fourteen, a couple of years ago, and she's wanted to come back ever since, but she just can't get away from her mother to go. She's planning on coming next year. I've got an exchange student that I had coming back from Germany to see it, hopefully, next year at the same time. So, the word is out. This place is well loved all over the world."

And just what is it that people love so much? "Camaraderie," Herb replies, "A lot of people meet old friends out here from different places," to which he adds, "The time of the year is a good time; it's not cold like Daytona is. It's just a great place to be. I love the country. And out of fifteen years I still have not seen all the sights. Sturgis is the only one I go to."

Leaning back, and switching his cane to his other hand, Herb elaborates on his personal rally itinerary. "I stay in Spearfish in this campground. I've been there for about seven years now; otherwise, I stayed at the KOA up there. And, I go down to Deadwood a lot – I love to gamble. Down to Rushmore, Keystone, Hill City. This year we went out to Custer Battlefield, so we get around to quite a few places. I've had some good experiences and I've had some bad. I can't say that I've ever come out here and gone home disappointed yet."

"You ride what you can afford, and you ride what you choose to."

Obviously, Herb has seen a lot of people come and go over the years, from gang members to millionaires. He believes that everybody, regardless of who they are or what they ride, belongs in Sturgis. "Even if you research your Hell's Angels," he observes, "some of them are doctors and lawyers, too. The biggest problem, years ago, was the Japanese-bike riders. You didn't get along, you weren't welcome here. But that has changed now – they're welcome, too. You ride what you can afford, and you ride what you choose to. And if someone else don't want to accept your choice, that's their problem." And if someone is not accepting, does that lead to trouble? "I can't say that I've seen really any trouble in all the years I've been here. I think I've seen maybe one fist fight. On the fiftieth I think they had one guy stab himself. Other than that, I can't say I've seen fights."

As with many of the regulars, the only thing he's seen that he doesn't quite understand is the young crowd riding their sports bikes. "I've seen a lot of your big crotch-rocket, high speed, high power jobs. I don't know why anybody wants them. Myself, I ride a Harley, but I ride for different reasons than those guys. They want to get out and crank it down the road at a hundred, hundred-and-ten. Fine, let'em. It's not my hide if they go down."

Ouch, going down on your bike. That's another matter that Herb can speak about. "I dumped my bike a couple years up at Mt. Rushmore. It wasn't serious, it was just a real unfortunate circumstance." Ironically, his spill in the hills didn't stop him from riding, but other unfortunate circumstances have. "Can't ride. I had surgery two years ago, and they kind of bummed my leg. I've been trying to get back up on the bike and get used to riding again. Hopefully, next year it will be here with me. I've got an '88 FLHS that I customized to full dresser – custom paint, chrome. Real nice looking machine. Got it right, paid for, stuck some money into it, and I got something worth something now. Like I say, hopefully next year. I've been on it, and I can move it around good. The leg is starting to come around a little bit, so hopefully next year it will be here."

"I'm just a home-made person...self-made boy, you know."

As you listen to Herb talk of his desire to ride again, you hear hopefulness, not bitterness, in his voice. It becomes clear that, while Herb may be a big man, he does not have a big attitude. With a quiet confidence, he refers to his black hat, black t-shirt, and bag full of new Harley duds, and admits, "365 days a year, this is me. The hair might get a little shorter once in a while, but that's about it. I've been riding since I was eight years old, and I've had this beard since I graduated in 1968. I'm just a home-made person…self-made boy, you know. I never had a lot of education. Didn't work real hard in school. I just had a few lucky breaks in the business world, so I've got myself a good job now. I'm happy, have just about everything I want. A couple nice kids. A good lady. Can't ask for much more."

That said, Herb gets up, balances, and makes his way down the street to enjoy the rest of the day.

NO
Please
Wipe
Your Feet
RALLY
QUARTERS
OPEN
p.m.
AIR
SHOP IN
COMFORT

JACKIE

"People can be themselves, and no one looks at you like you're weird or anything like that. You just have fun."

The most surprising thing about Jackie Thostenson is not her smile. Nor is it the studded, leather bikini bottoms she's wearing underneath her chaps. No, the most surprising thing about this 40-year-old elementary school teacher's aid - and mother of two teenage boys - from Brodhead, WI, is that Jackie is not a biker. She doesn't own a bike, and she's never been to Sturgis before. "I got invited out," she explains, "and I love Harleys, and I said, 'Sure, I'll go.'"

"I don't feel like I'm being distasteful, so I guess that's about it."

To her credit, Jackie has been to a few smaller rallies back in Wisconsin. She has friends who are members of ARM, the Association of Recovering Motorcyclists, and she has traveled a little with them. So, when the opportunity came to attend the Sturgis rally, it seemed like a good idea. "Just to say, 'I've been there, done that.' So you can see the bikes and the different people, and soak it all up."

As Jackie soaks up the rally, she has come to several conclusions about what makes Sturgis so popular. "People can be themselves, and no one looks at you like you're weird or anything like that. You just have fun. Sturgis is unique in itself; it's just got the freedom," she says, adding, "It's just been like 'Wow.' I guess I really like it at night with all the lights, and how everybody is just really into it. It's just a good time."

And Jackie's favorite thing to do? "Just walking the streets, and I love to people watch. That's my favorite thing to do – look at the bikes and just watch people." Of course, anybody on the street can tell you that just the opposite is happening – people are watching Jackie. Her good looks and sexy outfit are attracting attention. Many are lining up to take pictures. "Yeah, they're crowding around. And some of them want me to flash, but I'm not flashing – I'm not a flasher. I have a little taste. I don't care to do it." Flashing or not, Jackie admits that her attire is a little provocative. "I have to admit I was uncomfortable with it at first, but I just wanted to come out here and make it special, and have a good time."

She does admit that her "Special Sturgis look" was not entirely her idea. "My friend kind of prompted me to wearing this, and he said you'll fit right in. Even though I am dressed the way I am, I mean women do this, they still can have taste and still have a good time. I don't feel like I'm being distasteful, so I guess that's about it."

While Jackie may keep it tasteful, everybody knows that there are plenty of women in Sturgis who will flash their breasts for the camera. "The other women? All the power to them," Jackie exclaims. "If they want to do it, that's fine, let them do it. I mean, they're having fun. I have no problem with that."

Still on the subject of flashing, Jackie mentions that she has not been to any of the "wilder campgrounds" where that type of behavior is typical. "We were going to drive in one, but they had bands there, and they wanted to charge $27.00. We were just going to drive through, so we decided 'I don't think

so.'" So, she and her friend hit the local sights instead. "We've just been around Sturgis. We went to DeWitt today. We've been to Deadwood. We're staying at Mt. Rushmore, up by that way, and Crazy Horse. We did that Devil's Tower. Just touring, just going around."

> "I feel like with the professionals wanting to come out, letting loose and having a little fun, why not? I don't see anything wrong with that, of them wanting to do that."

In touring the vicinity, and seeing the crowds, Jackie has noticed the huge cross section of people who attend. "I see it as a good thing," she explains, giving some examples, "I feel like with the professionals wanting to come out, letting loose and having a little fun, why not? I don't see anything wrong with that, of them wanting to do that. I don't feel there is a dividing line there. I feel it's open to everybody who wants to do it. It doesn't matter – your job, or race, color, anything – it doesn't matter."

To Jackie, Sturgis is open to everybody. And that is one of the reasons she plans to come back. "And hopefully on my own bike," she adds. Currently, she doesn't ride, "But I'm going to. I've always enjoyed it, and I have a lot of friends that have Harleys, and I just love it. So hopefully, that will be my goal for next year, is to drive my own bike out here." To meet her goal, Jackie is taking the advice of many seasoned riders, and is planning to take a motorcycle training course. "Definitely. That's going to be a first. That's a given."

In the meantime, what else has this teacher's aid, mother, and provocative non-flasher been doing at Sturgis to get ready for the ride? "Actually," Jackie concludes demurely, "I've been riding the mechanical bull."

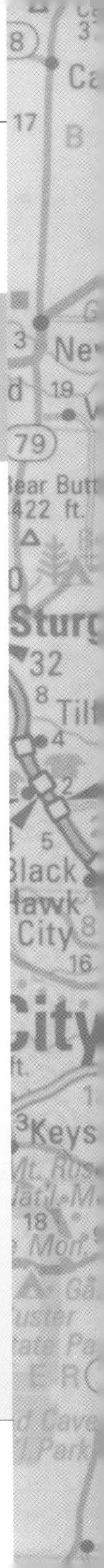

JAN

"I don't want to look at a map, I don't want to know where we're going, I don't ask...I just get on and ride."

"We're from Glenwood, Iowa," begins Janett Babb, age 56, "and I have a cleaning service there. That's what I do." Pointing to her husband, she adds, "John's retired." Then she points to the 2001 Custom motorcycle that she rode all the way to the rally. "It's a brand new custom that my husband built over the winter, and it rides like a dream. It's really a nice bike. The color turned out good and everything." Though riding her new bike out to Sturgis was a highlight of the rally for Jan, the downside occurred the night before, when an intoxicated rider ran into her prized possession while it was parked alongside their tent. "Somebody was just drunk, running around the campground here on his bike. I don't know what he was doing, but he ended up getting back behind a motor home and in through some picnic tables, and ran into my bike, my custom, unfortunately. Did some damage, could have been a lot worse – it wasn't any paint – it's all stuff you can replace, and that's good."

As John begins repairs on the damaged bike, Jan explains that this is their fifth time at Sturgis. They go to a few local poker runs back home, but don't attend other major rallies. As it is for so many, Sturgis is special for the Babb's. "I think it's the pretty riding. That's what we enjoy. That's what we come up here for, is to ride. We ride every day – almost all day, every day. We don't really participate in the other things that go on, but we like to ride and I like the scenery." While the landscape of the Black Hills is a draw for the Babb's, the commotion and congestion of downtown Sturgis is not.

> "That's what we come up here for, is to ride. We ride every day – almost all day, every day."

"Oh, we usually go once. We might do a little shopping there, or maybe take one day and go around Sturgis, but other than that we stay the heck out of there. It's a good place to stay away from."

The only other attraction they participate in during the rally is to watch the Harley drag races out by the Glencoe campground. "They're really, really good drags," Jan explains, but adds that even the best of drag strips isn't enough to keep them in that vicinity for an extended period of time. "We stayed at Glencoe for two or three years, and it just got wilder and wilder. You couldn't get any sleep, and it was a mess, you know, trash all over. We like it here because there's flush toilets and showers. It was a big selling point for me. It's cheap and it's quiet. I can hike back up here," she says, pointing to the hilltops behind her. "This is national forest, so I've been hiking up on top of that mountain."

Looking over the campground, one can't help but notice that the place is very open and airy, almost deserted. "I think it's down this year. Last year there was lots more, but that was the millennium. I was surprised that it dropped as much as it did, 'cause this campground isn't nearly as full as it was last year…but that's okay with us." Of course, a few more people wouldn't hurt. Jan knows that overall rally numbers are up, and she believes that there's plenty of room for everybody. "The Black Hills are big enough that you can spread people out all over it. It doesn't really matter how big it gets, 'cause they're spread all over. It's not like you've got 400,000 people in this campground."

> "There's more and more women riding all the time. There's no reason they can't ride, too."

Of course, it only took one person in the campground to run into Jan's custom motorcycle. That mishap, she feels, is the exception rather than the rule. "Most of the bikers are pretty careful," she says, though she does recognize the dangers that exist when dealing with younger riders on their crotch rockets. "They're the ones that are zipping in around you. I get a little concerned about that, a little worried about the safety factor. I don't think they have any idea what they're doing; they don't know what could happen. They're invincible, as far as they know. That worries me a little bit."

Continuing on, Jan contrasts that reckless riding style to her own reasons for riding a bike. "I think it's relaxing. It seems to me like as soon as I get on the bike – and I don't really have high blood pressure – but it's just like you can just feel it coming down, you know. You just really relax and you don't think about anything but riding – just going down the road. I like to follow him," she says, pointing again to her husband, "then I don't even have to think about where to turn or anything. I just follow him. I don't want to look at a map, I don't want to know where we're going, I don't ask…I just get on and ride. He never says 'Where do you want to go?' He just gets on and goes and I follow. That's kind of the way we like it."

Whether she leads or follows, Jan realizes that, as a woman rider on a classy custom bike, she stands out in a crowd. "A lot of people are really surprised.

They're also surprised that I'm a grandmother who rides her own bike. After you get to talking to them it isn't that big of deal – because it really isn't that big of deal. There's more and more women riding all the time. There's no reason they can't ride, too. They're probably safer riders than some of the guys; they're not as gutsy. And this bike is so much easier to ride than my Sportster that I just can't believe the difference. The Sportster's low, too, but it's got a different center of gravity. This one just flows with you. People are surprised, but not after I talk to them for a while – it's not a big deal."

"The Black hills are big enough that you can spread people out all over it."

Jan is quick to point out that who she is as a woman on a motorcycle is something different than the woman who is into flashing and exhibitionism on a bike. "Well, they're not usually on motorcycles on the front. Once in a while they are, but they're usually riding behind somebody. At first it kind of bothered me, but you just kind of blow it off after a while. Some people are going to do that anywhere if they can get away with it. I guess I wish they'd do less of it, but you know, it's life. The more people make of it, the more they're going to do it. It's not that big of deal." Jan's motorcycle attire is definitely more casual, subdued, and practical. "I wear the same stuff I wear at home. Everybody's got their t-shirts, and that's about all we do, same stuff. If you're riding, that's what we wear, so I don't really change to come out here."

Though Jan is confident in who she is as a woman and as a rider, she is reluctant to involve her grandchildren in her hobby. "They kind of want to do it. I'm a little bit hesitant, because it is a dangerous sport. There's no getting around it. You have no protection. Even though we wear helmets, that's it, that's all you've got, and any leather you have on. I feel like, if I want to ride and endanger myself, that's me, that's okay. I do what I can to protect myself, but to put somebody else on the back of my bike and then be responsible, I haven't gotten that far. They want to ride, but we're a little bit iffy about it so far." Still, the grandkids persist. Jan chuckles as she shares a story about her granddaughter. "She asked me the other day, 'Grandma, what are you going to do with the bikes when you get too old to ride?' I said, 'I don't know, I might have them buried with me.' She says, 'Think you could pass them down to me?'"

JERRY

"I'm really looking at the bikes. Looking at what's going on. I stay out of some of the wild campgrounds."

"This is going to be kind of a boring interview."

So says Jerry Ogstad, age 59, as he sits alone on a shaded side street, drinking an extra large lemonade and looking for relief from the 110 degree heat. He is waiting for his brother-in-law. The two men rode their motorcycles from Arizona to get to the rally. In a brief, simple, and understated manner – which one soon recognizes as trademark Jerry – he summarizes the two thousand mile journey across the country on his Harley-Davidson Road King, "Really pretty good. The last 500 miles was hot."

When you press him further, you discover that this quiet, "boring" man has a life history that few people can match. "I don't have an education. Never worked for a big company. I owned a couple of fishing boats in Alaska and commercial fished," he explains, once again understating his accomplishment, "When I went up there, I didn't know anything about it, but I learned. Learned good." After teaching himself the fishing trade, jobs and life changes took Jerry to Idaho, and finally to Arizona, where he owns and fixes rental properties in his semi-retirement.

"You get to see kind of everything here. That's kind of what I come for."

If Jerry finds nothing to brag about in himself, he finds plenty to brag about in his children. "They both got educations," he beams. His daughter completed college and now works as a high school teacher. His son finished a graduate degree and teaches college. "I'm happy of that," Jerry nods, "I'm a happy camper, there."

But right now, Arizona, and kids, and work, are thousands of miles away. Right now, it's time to enjoy Sturgis. "I'm really just looking at the bikes. Looking at what's going on. I stay out of some of the wild campgrounds. We do a little partying. Nothing drastic. See all the sights. Go to all the vendors, all that kind of stuff." Jerry has been to Sturgis three of the last four years. "This has been kind of the granddaddy of rallies. I go to Laughlin, 'cause I live in Arizona. Then I've been to a couple in California and around." When he compares the rallies, Sturgis stands out in terms of sheer size and personality. "More people. More, ah, different, people," he says, with a knowing wink, "You get to see kind of everything here. That's kind of what I come for. It's kind of fun to just sit and watch. Man, you can see everything. You know, you can see wealthy people dressed up like Harley people." He stops, laughs, and concludes, "Well, you can tell the newcomers."

And what of these newcomers? Do you really see that many wealthy "wanna-be's" at the rally? "A lot more than you used to. I've been riding bikes for years, but now you see a lot of that. Of course, that's what's making Harley-Davidson. That's what's making them now. Gees. That's changed." After a pause, Jerry's tone shifts slightly. "I actually think it's changed for the better. You know, it's kind of accepted. In the old days, I remember a couple years ago, gees, you were kind of a…kind of a ….if you rode a bike, then people would kind of shy away from you. It's a different world."

"Oh, the riding is great.
It's kind of fun.
A lot of people wave."

All and all, Jerry doesn't worry about excessive changes in the motorcycling lifestyle. "The old bikers will pretty well stay that way, you know, the old outlaw kind of guys. The other people, a lot of them do it for a while and then quit anyway. That's what I've seen." The other thing he's seen, and the thing that surprises him the most, is the amount of money some people spend on the activity. "Some of those guys ride $30,000-40,000 bikes up and down the street. And you know they didn't ride them here. They come in behind a motor home on a fancy trailer." Jerry goes on, describing a scene he recently witnessed at a local bike dealership, "There was a guy standing there, and they was going to buy three of 'em! And they start at about $33,000 and go to $45,000. The guy says 'Make us a deal on these three.' I mean, that's a hundred thousand dollars. You can't believe it."

Let them spend their money, Jerry thinks. As for he and his brother-in-law, they keep it simple. "We camp in tents. We eat out all the time 'cause cooking's not a good deal. We camp in somebody's back yard up here, and they have a bathroom and charge ten bucks a day." That's it. Simple pleasures. Living lean and, of course, riding. "Oh, the riding is great. It's kind of fun. A lot of people wave."

There are some advantages to being an uncomplicated man. It keeps you from complaining about what you don't have. It gives you time to focus on your children. And, for Jerry, it makes planning for the future pretty easy. He's already looking forward to riding from Arizona to Wisconsin in 2003 to celebrate the 100th anniversary of Harley-Davidson. "I'm going to Milwaukee to that. To that big one. My brother-in-law was there to the 95th, and he says people waved American flags and, you know, it just made the hair stand up on the back of his neck. So it was kind of neat. I'm going to the 100th."

Simple pleasures.

Joker

"Sturgis is not a stereotype. It's a gathering of people that are just looking to be connected, for whatever reason."

Michael "Joker" Warne had a dream. For most of his life, he wanted to go to the Sturgis rally. But the 45-year-old husband and father of two children could never get away. His addiction to drugs kept him at home. "I could never get out here – because of the disease. The concept of leaving my connection, or spending money I could have been spending on dope to come to Sturgis, just wasn't gonna happen."

Now, clean and sober for more than four years, Joker has finally arrived. Not only is he drug-free, he's president of the Cedar Rapids, IA, chapter of the Association of Recovering Motorcyclists. "That's a sober motorcycle association, started in LaCrosse 16 years ago, and now we've got chapters in Canada, Sweden, all over the 48 states, and one in Hawaii. There are more sober and clean bikers than you might think. A lot of times people don't change 'cause they see the light, they change 'cause they feel the heat. After living that lifestyle for so many years, it wears on you, it takes a toll. And the ones that want to get out, can. They have a choice."

Joining ARM was a major event in Joker's life. "It was another commitment I made to my recovery, to not using and abusing. I never felt like I fit in or I belonged and getting cleaned up, being sober, I still had that feeling of not belonging, and I was looking for something that I could belong to, where I fit in. I found ARM, and because I was a wing-nut and a loser, they took me in." Joker points out his shaved head, tattoos, and leather vest, and observes that he's more at peace as a "clean biker" than he was as an upstanding but addicted citizen. "I've come to realize – I don't ride because it's fashionable, I don't ride because it's cool. I ride because I like to ride, and the sense of freedom. I've been enlightened. That's what I'm about. Because I live life on life's terms and act like a productive member of society, that doesn't mean I have to wear khakis and loafers and have a certain haircut, or wear a certain designer label. There's no Clark Kent/Superman going on here, and that's what I was...that's the life that I lived when I was using. I had a double identity. I was a good employee – sport coat – when I was using, and then as soon as I went home from work I'd switch identities and I'd be a drug addict. I don't have to do that today."

Being clean has lead to some significant changes in Joker's life. "I've got a couple bucks in my jeans, and I don't have to worry about the cops pulling me over because I don't have a license, or I don't have insurance, or 'cause I'm holding. You can't pay for that – the feeling is just too good." Most important, Joker wants to spread that good feeling, and has taken a job that allows him to do just that. "I'm the program director of a transitional program for people in early recovery from chemical dependency. It's a private foundation supported by United Way. The residents have to pay a program fee to live there, and we take them right out of drug treatment, sometimes right out of corrections, occasionally off the street – you know, right out from under the bridge, and they can live there for up to eighteen months if they're willing to do the hard work necessary to change their lives. And after living under a bridge for fifteen years, it's a lot of work to integrate yourself back into the community, to become an acceptable, responsible member of society again. About a third of them are dual diagnosed, they also have a mental illness. Quite a few of them are on parole or probation. Basically, it's a homeless program, a transitional program. If you look at the hardcore homeless, fifty percent of them are mentally ill and fifty percent of them are chemically dependent, and there's a big overlap – and that makes up a hundred percent of the hardcore homeless, the people that are consistently without a home. It's 'Living Skills 101.' When they come in the door, it's a given they don't want to drink or use anymore, and now 'Hey, let's tune up those living skills.' Let's get you in a pattern of paying your bills, making your appointments on time, being accountable and doing the deal. You know, living life on life's terms. That's what we do."

"Since I got clean and sober, there is no us and them – it's just 'us.' It's people."

Listening to Joker's passionate explanation of what he does for a living, you become more and more pleased that he finally made it out to Sturgis. He deserves it. The funny thing is, he's out here now for completely different reasons than his original dream. "I've been riding motorcycle for a long time. This is probably my fifteenth, sixteenth year of riding. I always felt like this was the place to go. I'd hear stories. Originally, my motivation was coming here for the vice. You know, I was coming here for debauchery. I wanted to see flesh, and hang out with the real party animals. Now that I'm cleaned up and I actually have realized this goal, it's just awesome. For years and years and years I rode a motorcycle, and sold drugs, and carried a gun, and – because it wasn't the right kind of motorcycle, I felt like I was a wanna-be or a 'fringe.' And that's the nature of having the disease of addiction, too."

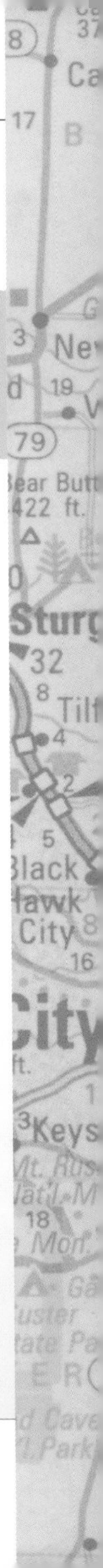

How ironic. There sits Joker, looking completely at home in this environment, yet for years he viewed himself as an outsider because he didn't ride the "right kind of motorcycle." In other words, he didn't have a Harley. "Now that I'm no longer using my twisted perception I realize this - that it's not what you ride, it's a lifestyle." And Joker's lifestyle choice right now is BMW, specifically, a 1998 BMW R1200. "One of the unwritten laws is you never see a BMW on a trailer. It's not a German Shepard, it doesn't like riding in the back of pickup trucks. And I ride 14,000 miles a year, so it's important to me to ride the whole way out here."

Now imagine this. Here's a man who dreamed for years of coming to the Sturgis rally. He finally defeats his drug addiction, and plans to ride a motorcycle – one that doesn't like trailers – from Cedar Rapids, IA all the way to Sturgis. So what happens? Halfway across South Dakota Joker's bike breaks down. "And it's electrical, and I'm not the guy to fix it. I couldn't ask any of the Harley riders to fix it, 'cause they don't know how to fix them either." Is this the end of the dream? Was the lifelong fight for nothing? "I'm so blessed," Joker says, "I rode out here with some recovering people, and they had their bikes on trailers. So we took one bike off, and put my bike on. My ARM brother said, 'Here, you ride mine.' So I got my wish, I got to ride all the way to Sturgis first time." Now that's a story.

> "You know, living life on life's terms. That's what we do."

And now that he's here, Sturgis is everything he hoped it would be. In fact, it's probably better. Once, he was looking for the vice. He was on the outside looking in. His addiction separated him from many and put him at odds with the system. Now, his view of the rally is sobering – no pun intended – and deeply philosophical. "Since I got clean and sober, there is no us and them – it's just 'us.' It's people. It's not the system, it's not law enforcement, it's not politicians, it's just people. It's all about human beings, not about systems. I used to be us and them. Us was the drug users, and them was anybody that wanted to get in the way of us using drugs. Today, it's just us. Everybody's got a job to, and we're all just trying to make it."

"Sturgis is not a stereotype." Joker concludes, "It's a gathering of people that are just looking to be connected, for whatever reason. I'm sure some people's motivation is less than pure, but it's a beautiful thing. It's an opportunity to see people you'd never see, maybe do some things you'd never do, and enjoy a part of the country that's just awesome. I'm tickled. I'm so blessed, my life couldn't be any better."

STURGIS
"00"

JUDY

"We have three bikes, but I don't ride. I like being a passenger. I like being able to watch everything as we go by and check it all out."

This is Judy Croteau's first time at Sturgis. You'd never guess it from her attire. Everything matches. Black on black with red rose inlays, right down to her boots.

The main reason Judy hasn't been to Sturgis before is because of its distance from home. She and her husband are from South Florida, and the drive up was a killer. Back home, Judy's husband drives a truck, so he is accustomed to the long haul. Judy works as an elementary school substitute teacher, and serves as director of the local Boys and Girls Club. Wonderful jobs, but they don't really prepare you for a cross country journey.

They drove up from Florida with another couple, one vehicle towing a camper, the other towing their bikes. "I wanted to see the mountains and ride through them. And go over to Deadwood. It's really nice, but I prefer Daytona. We go to Daytona all the time. You see a lot more bike-wise. You know, the bike dealers, the bike builders. There's a lot more there. This is more Harley. There it's everything…a little bit of everything…and I like that."

"It's really nice, but I prefer Daytona. We go to Daytona all the time."

In fact, the emphasis on Harley-Davidson in Sturgis was another possible drawback of the trip. You see, Judy rides as a passenger on the back of her husband's Kawasaki. "I was worried about coming to a place that was all Harleys, and we're not driving one. Sometimes you can get a crowd that's not too friendly because you're not driving a Harley." After a while, Judy realized that the Sturgis crowd was nothing to worry about. "This place is very friendly, though. People are really, really nice. Daytona, they're friendly, but not as friendly. Sturgis is a very friendly place."

"We're staying at a campground," she says, giving an example, "There's a big shower room, and all the ladies are in there and, you know, it's like 'Hi. Hi. How are you? Where are you from?' And you're walking down to your campsite and the guys stop and talk to you. We went out yesterday for the day and there was a kind of, I guess, a little storm. We came back and they had closed up our camper for us – just neighbors that we hadn't even met. I mean, that was fantastic. Nothing blew away."

Even if Sturgis is "not quite Daytona," Judy and company found plenty to do. "We went out to Main Street. I liked it, walking by and looking at all the bikes and the people. I like people watching – what they wear, how they talk, where they're from. We went to Deadwood last night to gamble. That was fun. I enjoyed that. We hit quite a few casinos. We walked up and down and went into all the stores. Very expensive, but anything like this you're going to see that."

As she walked and rode around, Judy couldn't help but notice two of the groups that more and more seem to define the Sturgis experience – the corporate bikers and the female flashers. She's pretty open minded about both.

"People can do what they want to do. If they're friendly, they don't bother me. That's fine with me. I can go with the flow." Regarding the upscale riders, she emphatically states, "I don't care if you're a lawyer or if you're a ditch digger. Makes no difference to me." And the exhibitionists? "If you're well proportioned and you want to show a little bit, that's fine. There's nothing wrong with that. But when you're a horror show – keep it on. Look in a mirror before you go out. If you've got it and you want to flaunt it, more power to you. Don't bother me any."

"People can do what they want to do. If they're friendly, they don't bother me."

Maybe it's Judy's ability to "go with the flow" that makes her so comfortable with her brand of motorcycle riding. Judy is now, and always will be, a passenger. "I love it," she quips, "We have three bikes, but I don't ride. I like being a passenger. I like being able to watch everything as we go by and check it all out." Pointing to her husband, she adds "He tries to get me to ride, but I don't want to. No way."

Regardless of whether or not Judy sits at the front or back of the bike seat, she still really, really looks the part. She explains that the matching gear was a gift her husband purchased at – where else? – the Daytona rally. She explains, however, that this is rally attire only, and is not how she dresses back at home. "Nah, nah, not at all. I'm a substitute teacher, so I dress up."

In fact, the biker look is so foreign to Judy's regular style that many people, her three children included, are surprised that she would come to the Sturgis rally at all. "They can't believe I went," she says, referring to her kids, "Even at school I'm telling them I'm going to Sturgis and they're looking at me like 'Really? You?' I say, yeah, I'm going to go, see what it's like." And what will she tell them when she gets home? "It's nice. I'm glad I came, but I think it will be a while before I come back. Only because of the ride."

MICKEY
MICKEY
MICKEY
MICKEY
GENUINE LEATHER

KAREN LOUISE

"I think I'd like to see more people from outside America coming to Sturgis, and to see this bizarre, awesome experience, and hopefully take it back to their country and do something there."

"Every year during college when I was back home in the UK," says Karen Louise Malsbury in her crisp British accent, "I used to come out here and au pair for three different families." Now a 23-year-old graduate student at Oakland University in Michigan, the former resident of Worcester in the United Kingdom has traveled to Sturgis to visit a former host family who runs a leather store during the rally. "Every year they used to come out here and set up their shop, and come home with the pictures and the video evidence. And this year I was given the opportunity now that I've moved to Michigan, and so, yep, I'm here enjoying and having fun. It's great!"

"Currently, I'm doing a Masters degree in Education," Karen Louise continues, "Secondary Education. My major is in Information Technology and my minor is in Geography. At the moment, with my husband's job, we've got a three-year Visa here – therefore, we'll stay here for three years and see how we get on. If it's extended, then that's the better for us. If not, we go back home, or we may move on to Australia or Japan with his industry, which is the car industry. But with my degree, I hope to get back into education as soon as possible."

Interestingly enough, the rally actually feels a little bit like home. "It's my first time in Sturgis. It's a crazy, crazy party atmosphere. Much like the festivals we have back home in the UK. During the summer months we have huge, huge festivals – open air, with lots of mud usually due to the rain. And you just go to the gigs and you just hang out, and get really, really dirty, and go home and regret what you've done for the last couple of days. But, that's what fun, so you get on with it."

"It's a crazy, crazy party atmosphere. Much like the festivals we have back home in the UK."

"I just believe it's a way of getting like-minded people together," she continues, "to enjoy, and to show off a little, and to have fun and let your hair down. And these people are on vacation, and they 'enjoy' from 6 o'clock in the morning when it's too hot to be in their tent 'til 3 o'clock at night when they're pushed off the streets because they need to clean the streets. They just enjoy. It's great." Compared to home, one difference she's noticed about Sturgis is, "There's lots of naked people. They like to expose themselves a little bit more than necessary."

Well, some of the people might be naked, but at least they're not dangerous. "I feel confident here walking down the street on my own. If you bump into someone, they apologize immediately. I just feel so safe. And if I left my camera on the curb there," she says, pointing to the motorcycle-lined street in front of the store, "if I came back an hour later it'd still be there. If you look along the back of these bikes, there's helmets, there's new leather jackets that have just been purchased, there's camping gear, there's everything that you could ever need. And it stays there."

As she hangs around and lends a hand at her friend's leather store, Karen Louise begins to describe the variety of people she meets day after day. "I've met doctors, lawyers…and you know, they don't look like doctors and lawyers. They change their appearance drastically to come here – to fit in, to conform. And then you meet people traveling around the country, and they've been to places I've never heard of. Their life is just to travel with their bike, and just to see places you would not see if you were just a general tourist or backpacker." Despite all the different walks of life she encounters, she hasn't noticed any trouble caused by the diversity. "I don't see it as a problem. They seem to just kind of hang out together, listen to each other's stories, and just appreciate what they're saying – or they have their own opinions and they just step back. They have a sheer love for bikes and anything that has to do with it, whether it's leather, whether it's to do with hairstyles, tattoos, whatever. They have an interest, and if you can put your story across, and it's interesting and it's worth listening to, I think that's where they have their similarities."

The best proof Karen Louise has to support her claim that everybody in Sturgis gets along comes from her own experience of meeting people from her own country. "I met some British people earlier today, and they did not look to me like middle-class British people coming over here. They were from London. Some of them didn't have teeth, some of them were so burnt that their skin was all red and blistering. Ordinarily, if they were at home walking down the street, I wouldn't have spoken to them. But because they were here at Sturgis, and the fact that they're British,

I wanted to know where they were from, what they did, and what brought them here. They were just having an awesome time, and they bought chaps and stuff and they've never ridden before. They just wanted to go home and have a memento. They were just here to enjoy, so that was cool."

"If you bump into someone, they apologize immediately. I just feel so safe."

Leather chaps for non-motorcycle riding, sunburned partiers from London. What else gets sold at the store? "We have some jackets that you can just wear to the mall, you know, just out regularly, out and about. And then we have like biker jackets here. You get a cross-section." And does Karen Louise wear the goods herself? "There's no way," she proclaims firmly, then pauses and adds, "The other day I was asked, because I was the same size as someone's wife, to put on a bodice leather top, and did so because I was kind of egged into it. But it soon came off 'cause it's too hot to wear leather…it's way too hot."

Despite the heat, the annual rally is something Karen Louise would recommend for everybody – everywhere. "I think I'd like to see more people from outside America coming to Sturgis, and to see this bizarre, awesome experience, and hopefully take it back to their country and do something there. I've met people from Australia, Holland, South Africa, so, yeah, we're getting there, but it'd be nice to have something on this scale elsewhere around the world. I'm just lucky to have the opportunity to come out here."

To Karen Louise, Sturgis is both entertaining and educational. "I have been out to Mt. Rushmore and seen some of the countryside. That's part of my study in Geography. Just to see the landscape is awesome, breathtaking." She considers herself especially fortunate to be here, knowing that she and her sunburned countrymen are the exception rather than the rule. "You don't usually come out this far, if you're going to come from Britain, on vacation. It's usually Miami, Chicago, New York, L.A.," she concludes. "You know, you don't say, 'Well, I need a flight to Rapid City.'"

Harley-Davidson
JESUS

Keydude & Kim

"You can't condemn them for what they do, unless you expect them to condemn you for what you do."

The last time Ken "Keydude" Putnam, age 48, was at the Sturgis rally was in 1975. Back then he was here to party; to use and abuse. This time he has returned with his 40-year-old wife Kim – her first trip to Sturgis - with a very different mission. A mission from God. "We're up here with the Christian Motorcyclists Association to minister."

The evangelist couple hails from Kaufman, Texas, about fifty miles east of Dallas. Keydude, well nicknamed since he is a locksmith, rode his 1989 Harley-Davidson FLHS, while Kim, an accounting clerk, trailered her 1980 Harley-Davidson FLH Shovelhead. They have belonged to the CMA for about four years. "We belong to the prison team ministry," Keydude explains, but mentions they may be shifting their pastoral focus. "I'm going to join the mechanical team," he says, and Kim, in her soft Southern drawl, adds that she may become part of the Servant team.

Keydude reflects on the changes in his life since his last visit to the rally in the mid-70's. "When I was here before, I was a secular individual, not religious. It was an entirely different experience. My opinion then of a good time was very different. Last time I was here I was strung out on drugs. I drank. I partied. The whole nine. I still got a motorcycle, I still love to ride, but now my high is the Lord. He provides what I need. I don't need the other party. I don't condemn those that do, but to each their own. You can't condemn them for what they do, unless you expect them to condemn you for what you do."

He also reflects on the changes in Sturgis itself. "It's neutral now. Last time I was here, it was either 'You're a biker, or you're a wanna-be.' There was no compromise. There was very little repertoire, so to speak. There was no talking. 'Get away from me. You're a weekend warrior. I don't have time for you.' Now it's not like that. Now it's a bunch of people, with a bunch of motorcycles, all with the same outlook on life – they love to ride. Bottom line – love to ride. Just my opinion, people are really motorcycle people. The one-percenter, per se, a thing of the past, just like the ducktail. I think it's just the dawn of a new generation."

This new generation, Keydude adds, sure adds to the size of the crowd "Gotten big. Now, it's more of a public event other than a quote 'motorcycle event.' It's become very commercialized.

It's all about money now instead of a good time. Other than that, it's still great." Kim likes the way Sturgis operates now, compared to stories she used to hear. "I think it's a positive thing. Used to, you'd be afraid to walk down through there, but now, it's a little bit more laid back, there's more control. More than anything I like the control. I was afraid there was going to be a lot of rowdy behavior, stuff that I really didn't want to see. I have seen some stuff that I didn't want to see, but not quite as bad as I thought it would be. I think it's great."

"I still got a motorcycle, I still love to ride, but now my high is the Lord."

– *Keydude*

Keydude agrees. "It's becoming a family event, which is a great thing, it really is. You've got so many little kids, all they know is what they hear about Sturgis, what they hear about motorcycle riders, negative publicity on TV. Only thing you ever hear about a motorcycle club on television is negative aspect, most generally. Robbing, stealing…and that's so negative, 'cause there's more to it than that, so much more."

Of course, both Keydude and Kim know that the rowdy party element still exists, particularly in some of the more infamous campgrounds on the outskirts of town. "Everybody makes a choice," Kim says, "Hopefully, one day they'll decide to take the other path. But everybody has to make their own choice. Sometimes the hard road is the best way to get to your right choice." Her choice is to stay away from the party spots. They're staying at a chuch-based campground instead. "Foothills Baptist Church," Ken explains, "Real nice people there at that church. CMA members will all be camping free. We even have shower access, air conditioning inside the building, telephone if we needed it. They've been excellent." To this, Kim adds, "It was a blessing."

Speaking of blessings, and this couple frequently does, Keydude shares the following. "It's been a blessing to me to be back up here again. It's an entirely different lifestyle that I've come in this time. And it just reconfirms why I'm doing this now, because I don't want to be there no more…I'm not that person anymore."

What Keydude and Kim really hope is that other troubled bikers can learn the same lesson he has; that they can change if they want to. And being members of the CMA allows the Putnams to open up conversations with the people they meet. "They want to know just basic information," says Kim, "Where's the church around here? How can I get in touch with the CMA? What do you'all do? Stuff like that." Keydude nods, adding, "That's the biggest question, 'What's CMA about?' It's about saving souls. It's bringing people to the Lord, one person at a time."

Kim describes how it works, and who she talks to. "People that you can't normally touch, because they are a rough crowd, and if you've yourself been there, they relate more to you than they do a preacher walking through there preaching. You can talk to them on a one to one level. You don't have to talk about Jesus, and they may just bring it up." She continues, describing her typical witnessing encounter, "I personally encounter mostly the hardcore. They're searching, that's the reason they're hardcore. They're searching for something, and they just haven't found the right path. And if you're there to help them out, set them on the right path, plant the seed – and somebody else might come along and water it."

"Sometimes the hard road is the best way to get to your right choice."

– *Kim*

Keydude chips in, adding a recent example. "Last night we had a fellow CMA'er, actually the president of our chapter, and another member was downtown, cruising, so to speak. And this young couple come up, they was probably I'd say mid-twenties, and we sat there and ministered to them - fellowship – just talking, you know, just one on one. And before they left, the guy hit his knees and give his heart to the Lord. So did his wife." Keydude chokes with emotion as he describes the scene. "It just rips you apart to see what you can do, and you don't have to try – just be there."

"The problem they have is pride," Keydude goes on. "They don't want their buddy to see them talking to a Jesus biker. That's not cool. When they can swallow that pride, you know that

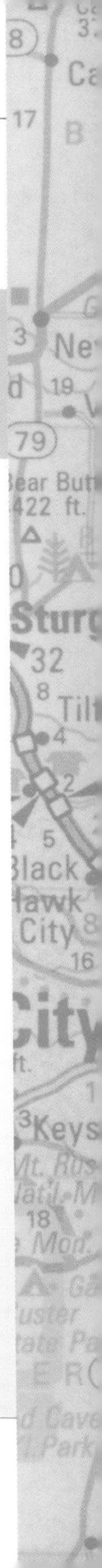

> "I was afraid there was going to be a lot of rowdy behavior, stuff that I really didn't want to see. I have seen some stuff that I didn't really want to see, but not quite as bad as I thought it would be."
>
> *– Kim*

they're hurting inside, but you know they're interested or they wouldn't do it in front of their friends." Of course, not all bikers – no matter how much they are searching – are ready to swallow that pride. So the Putnams get a little grief now and then from the people they meet. "A lot of flack, sometimes," admits Keydude, and then he and Kim provide a duet of the various negative responses they receive.

"Why don't you just go away and leave me alone. I'm not interested."

"Or, 'Here comes those Jesus freaks."

"There's those Jesus people again."

Keydude tries to clarify their evangelical goals and strategies. "A lot of times we're viewed as like...oh, what do they call them…the people that run the tracts around at your door all the time…Jehovah's Witnesses. We're confused quite often with that type of religious prayer. CMA, to me is not, 'Look, I want to talk to you about God. Let me have some of your time.' It's not like that at all. 'Hey, bro, what's up?' Let them deal the hand from there. If they want to talk about it, talk about it. If they don't, just talk."

Kim nods in enthusiastic agreement. "God will put that there. If it's in their mind and in their heart, He'll strike it for you." It is just that opportunity, that possibility, that brought them to the place called Sturgis. "I guess it's just the name, the reputation," Kim continues, "And the thought of maybe winning that one soul. It's great. It makes you feel really wonderful when you actually do touch somebody."

Happily, it's not all work and no play for the Putnams. They also take some time to do the touristy things. "We went up to Mt. Rushmore, the Iron Mountain Trail," says Kim. Keydude puts his arms around his wife's shoulder. "First riding she'd ever done in any hill

country, and she was awesome." Kim puts her arm around her husband's waist, and teasingly talks about the rest of their trip. "Can't spend no more money. Just take a couple of rides, maybe visit some caves."

Standing there, arms around each other, the Texan husband and wife evangelical team are the picture of happiness – the perfect motorcycle couple. "I wish everybody could be as blessed as we've been," Keydude prays, "Someday they will be."

A Bottle

LISA

"So I found a tail, and I hung it off my blue jeans. Sure enough, it caught people's attention. It just kind of became a trademark."

YOU DON'T NEED BIG BOOBS TO GIVE A GOOD MASSAGE, JUST BIG HANDS. So reads the sign above Lisa Peters' vendor booth. As if she needs the sign to grab people's attention. What most people notice about the 35-year-old massage therapist from New Hampshire is the raccoon tail attached to the back of her bare-bottomed leather chaps.

Lisa has been giving massages at motorcycle rallies for the past five years. Currently, she charges twenty dollars for a fifteen minute massage. That wasn't always the case, as Lisa explains what led up to her current practice and prices. "I had taken a seminar to do seated massage technique, and part of the seminar requirements were, once you took the course, you had to get 100 names on a sheet of people you'd worked on and mail it to California, where they check and make sure you've done all your work. I used to go to the rally in Laconia, New Hampshire, 'cause that's in my backyard. The first year I brought my massage chair was 'cause I had signatures to get. The second year I did it, everybody's like 'Let me give you some money.' 'No, I'm just doing this for fun. I got my signatures. I'm certified in this technique. I'm just doing it 'cause I like to.' And people insisted on giving me money for it. So then I'm thinking, well, gees, why not. Everyone here needs some work. So the following year I got a vending space and my vending license, and that started the ball rolling."

> "The bikers are very respectful, very trustworthy. Even the patch-wearers."

For those interested in starting such a business, be advised that the revealing outfit is not part of the certification. That's a personal choice. "It started with the tail," Lisa explains, "When I was in Laconia my first year, I was up on the top of a hill, in a large area where there was a lot of vendors. But I was new, and people weren't wanting to walk up the hill because there was no shade, and nobody wanted to haul their assess up there in the middle of the day. So I thought, 'I got to do something to catch their attention.' So I found a tail, and I hung it off my blue jeans. Sure enough, it caught people's attention. It just kind of became a trademark. If I go out at night without the tail on…'Hey, where's the tail?' It's all in good fun."

Lisa's outfit is attracting particular attention today. It's Tuesday in Sturgis, and so far it's legal for women to go topless as long as their breasts are painted. Yes, painted. "I had heard you couldn't show anything and you have to be covered, and blah, blah, blah," Lisa says, accenting her statement with a slight flip of the wrist, "And then I saw the little Budweiser girls running around with airbrushing the other day and I was like 'I got to check this out.' As long as they can't see the color of your nipples, you can walk around like this. So I'll push the boundaries." By Wednesday, Sturgis officials determined that airbrushed torsos pushed the boundaries a little too far, and declared the practice illegal. What does Lisa do when no airbrush artist is available or allowed? Smiling coyly, she explains, "I do have some rather nice leather tops that I wear."

Back home, minus the tail or the leather tops, Lisa has an office in a chiropractic clinic. Despite her thriving seven-year-old business there, and an established clientele, Lisa admits, "I love to be on the road. The thing with rallies is it's a great way to travel and see the country." When she can, she travels on her 1982 Harley-Davidson FXR. Currently, the bike is at home, and she's traveling with a vendor couple who work rallies as their primary source of income. "I'm home for a week and a half. Take care of as many people as I can out of my office. See my cat. Pay my bills. Say hi to my housemate. And then I'm on the road again."

This is the first year that the road has taken Lisa to the Sturgis rally, and so far she is pleased with what she sees. "It's real pretty out there. The crowd is a whole lot more relaxed out here than they are in some areas like New York and New Hampshire." The only drawback is that her work, which usually begins at 10:00 a.m. and continues until 11:00 p.m., doesn't always allow her time to play. "Because I work such long days, I don't really get the time to like go to the campgrounds and see the concerts or anything. I'd like to come my first three years and just work, and then one year I'll come and just be a spectator."

Until then, you won't catch Lisa complaining about the hours. People need her help, and she loves to help them. "Doesn't matter how you got here, whether you rode it, trailered it, flew it…there's tension. From your workday, or your playing, sleeping on the ground…everybody needs the work… and I love what I do. I could be in this for the money, but I'm not. I just like being out in the crowd. Everybody thinks the crowd feeds off me, but I feed off them as much as they feed off me. I can work a thirteen hour day and not be tired at the end of it."

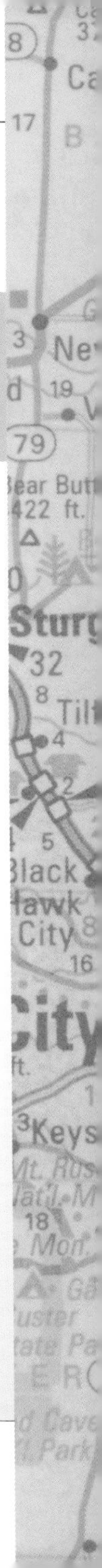

"I could be in this for the money, but I'm not. I just like being out in the crowd."

The only thing that Lisa does tire of is the treatment she gets from some of the younger riders. "What do you call them – the dot.com crowd. They're arrogant and unappreciative of anybody," she reports. "Any of the vendors will tell you that. We were brought up to be appreciative of people who were out working with the public. They don't have any respect for themselves; they don't respect other people or their properties. Those are the kids that are going to steal. Those are the kids that are going to be arrogant, completely rude, and just downright ignorant. They have no respect. That was the crowd that rolled in to the last part of Laconia this year, and every one of the vendors was fed up with them. They're the ones who will come up and grab me. They're the ones who will make comments to me."

Lisa compares these behaviors with those of the hardcore and grizzled bikers. "The bikers are very respectful, very trustworthy. Even the patch-wearers. I've never had a problem with them. They watch out for me when I'm on the road, 'cause typically I travel alone. If I need anything, 'You just tell us. We'll have it here in an hour.' They appreciate the fact that I'm independent, that I'm a hard worker, and that if I've got something to say I'll say it. I don't care whether you're wearing a patch or not."

Lisa looks at her watch, then turns back to her chair, her tail following her with a furtive flip. A small crowd has gathered. Some just want to take pictures. No problem. "I mean, it's a body. If they think it looks good, I'm flattered." Others are there for a massage. Smiling and welcoming the next customer, she goes back to work.

MAD MAX

"I've been on Main Street twice – that's enough. Too crowded. I like open spaces."

At a gas station just outside of town, two men overhear that interviews are being conducted for a book about Sturgis people. One man says, "You gotta talk to my wife. She is exactly the person you're looking for." Unfortunately, she is not with them. The three had been out for a morning ride but, when the two men stopped for gas, she didn't need any. And, since she would rather ride than wait, the last thing they saw was her taillight heading down the interstate.

Anticipating that she may have returned to the farm house they were renting, the husband rushes off to make a phone call. Within five minutes, Colleen Reynolds roars into the parking lot on her 1999 Harley-Davidson Softail Custom. Back home in Jarrettsville, Maryland, the 51-year-old mother of three and grandmother of two may be called "Grandma" (actually, "me-ma" from one of the grandkids), but at Sturgis – she is "Mad Max."

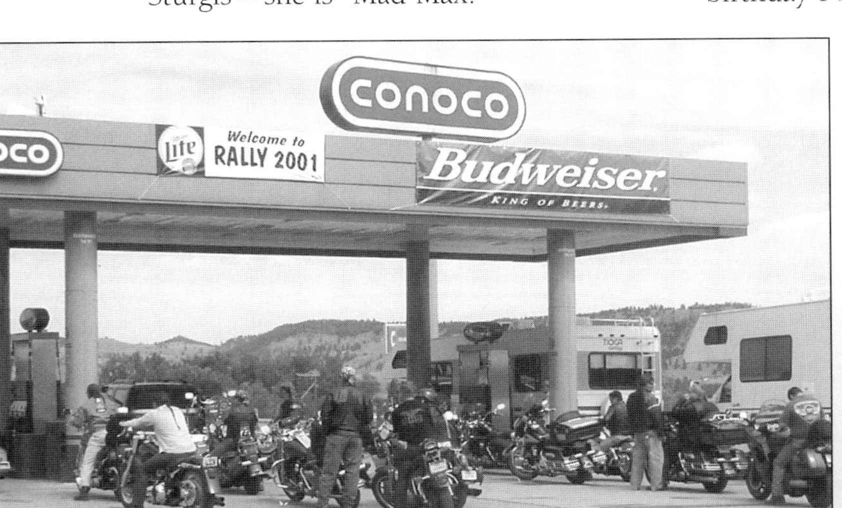

Mad Max is a recent returnee to the sport of motorcycling. "I rode back in the late sixties; started a motorcycle club," she explains. "Got out of that. Got married. Had kids, raised the kids. They're grown and gone. I've always wanted a Harley, and for my fiftieth birthday I bought myself a 1200 Sportster." Mad Max topped off her birthday purchase with her first tattoo – a picture of an Indian to celebrate the fact that she's part Native American. But it didn't stop there. "I've always wanted a Softail, and on my birthday this year in July I went and picked up my Softail."

Once the decisions were made to ride and get tattooed, going to rallies just naturally followed. She started at the Daytona rally in Florida, but wasn't very impressed. "I won't go back to Daytona. It's way too crowded. This is a lot more open, spread out – open spaces. You can go anywhere." Not only was the Florida rally more crowded, she continues, the people in the crowd were tough to deal with. "In Daytona, the spring break college kids – we overlapped, and it was horrible. The kids nowadays have no respect. The kids have no respect whatsoever. I haven't seen that out here. I've seen very few of the younger generation. I would say it's mostly my age…a little younger, a little older."

"I choose to ride – that's why I'm here."

After the disappointing turn of events in Daytona, Mad Max turned her sights to the Sturgis rally. This is her first time here. "Heard a lot about it. It's open; it's more open. There's places to go, more things to see. Love the great outdoors. This place is phenomenal – absolutely phenomenal." Best of all, Sturgis offers some of the things she likes to do best. "Just ride and shop." But not necessarily downtown. "I've been on Main Street twice – that's enough. Too crowded. I like open spaces." So she and her companions spend much of their time biking in the surrounding communities, enjoying the pleasantries of the Black Hills. "Just the ride. The atmosphere. The people. Just the whole place."

After a while, her experience at the rally sounds almost too good to be true. No problems or conflicts? "I haven't seen any at all. Everybody's been very, very friendly and nice." What about the social and income differences? Any boundary lines drawn there? "Not at all. No lines. I feel everybody's welcome…everybody." Even those riding something other than a Harley-Davidson? "I don't discriminate." And what about all those women flashing their breasts? Well, there might be a little problem there. "I don't think they're here for…what's the word I want to use…I don't think they're here for bike week. They're here to see what they can get. It's not about the motorcycles – especially the girl we saw on Main Street last night. She was built like a brick you-know-what, on a big trike. She had a thong on, a white leather thong, and…she had hardly nothing on. That's not bike week. She was really a pretty girl…she didn't do anything for me. Of course, you saw every man on Main Street taking pictures of her. I mean, if that's what she wants to do, that's her choice. I choose to ride – that's why I'm here."

> "What you see is what you get. I hold no punches. This is me. This is it."

All things considered, everything is going so well that Mad Max decided to commemorate her trip by adding what is now her third tattoo. This time it's a peace sign. "I'm a peace-loving person," she explains. One must remember, however, that being peace-loving doesn't mean that you're a pushover, or that you let other people tell you how you should look or act. Mad Max will have none of that. "What you see is what you get. I hold no punches. This is me. This is it. I can look like this, and if we go out to a nice restaurant, I can get dressed up in a $400 suit, in heels and pantyhose – but this is me. Jeans and a t-shirt. This is it."

And that makes sense. When you add it all together – love for the outdoors, peaceful feelings, and a personal sense of style that no one can take away – you have all the ingredients for a certain type of person. For a biker. "It's...freedom. That's what it means to me...freedom. If I get stressed, I get on my bike and ride. If I'm not happy about something, I get on my bike and ride." Fortunately, Sturgis is just the place for Colleen Reynolds, a.k.a. Mad Max, to experience that freedom.

"I feel like Peter Fonda in 'Easy Rider,'" she jokes. Then, taking a moment to scan the horizon and breathe in the air, she smiles and concludes, "I'll come back here."

SKULL CAPS $5.00 EA
CYLINDER EXCHANGE STATION
RALLY SPECIAL! $5.00 EA.
HAVE A GOOD DAY! RIDE SAFELY!
CUSTOM SKULL CAPS MADE IN U.S.A. BY LAVONNE (KENTUCKY)
"LadyLuvons"
AMERICAN MADE
Doo Ragz
Leather Goods
ETC.
WHOLESALE INQUIRES WELCOME

MAGOO

"We're both retired, we both like to travel, so she got the sewing machine out and she started making these things, and here we are."

Jack "Magoo" Backus has been riding motorcycles for over fifty-eight years. "Since 1942. I was on a motor scooter when I was I twelve years old. I'm seventy now, I'm an old man. I rode competition on a half-mile dirt track in the Midwest back in the late fifties. I've been to Laconia a few times; I've raced there a couple times – drag racing. It's just something that grows with me – I just love it."

No more racing for Magoo these days. Now, instead of doing the drags at rallies, the Ft. Myers, Florida resident does "doo ragz" instead. Leaning against a box of five dollar rally specials, proudly advertised as American Made, Magoo explains the work history which preceded his current sales career. "I was a motorcycle dealer years ago, and I was a machinist. I retired about ten years ago. I decided to go to school again to learn mechanics - repaired outboard motors and stuff in semi-retirement. I still do it now and then just for something to do, but I don't have time now."

He doesn't have time because of his seamstress friend Lavonne, a.k.a. "Lady Luvon." "I met this lady on the internet last year. She's knows I was wearing one of these skull caps – do rags – whatever you call it. She said, 'Jack, I can make you one of those.' I said, 'Okay, make me one.' She made me one; she made me a couple. My friends liked them; she made them also. We're both retired, we both like to travel, so she got the sewing machine out and she started making these things, and here we are."

"They're from all walks of life nowadays. A nicer element nowadays."

Magoo (so nicknamed because of actor Jim Backus, who was the voice of the cartoon Mr. Magoo and who played the millionaire Thurston Howell on "Gilligan's Island") has only been to Sturgis twice, and this is his first time here as a vendor. "Last year, I was here as a spectator. This year it's this." Sturgis is just part of the rally tour that he and new partner Lavonne travel to. "We were at Laconia a month, and sold quite a few of them. This is the second one this year. We're from Florida. We're going back to Florida in October for Daytona."

The fact that they sell a lot is not surprising. At five dollars apiece, "Lady Luvons doo ragz" are approximately one-third the cost of their mass produced competitors.

"When it comes to a large rally like this, it's all neutral territory. They all get along."

When he's not selling, Magoo and his 1996 Harley-Davidson Sportster are doing one of the things he loves the best. "Riding. My wife, she rides with me." Then he pauses, realizing he has gotten ahead of his story. "I said my wife," he winks, "actually, not yet – we're working on it."

And what better place to work on it than Sturgis? "I like the scenery – the hills, the riding – it's a beautiful place to ride." Standing there in his tank top, shorts, unzipped ankle boots, and–of course–a Lady Luvon skull cap, Magoo seems a part of the scenery himself. He looks, well, comfortable; like he belongs. "People complain about the heat," he observes. "Doesn't bother me, 'cause I'm from Florida anyhow. It's a dryer heat here, it seems to me. I can tolerate it better."

The only thing Sturgis needs, Magoo feels, is a little more of his old hobby – dirt track racing. "But that's my opinion. I mean, they've got a couple nights of it. Last year I was here they had one night of short-track and one day of half-mile." When he does get to the races, he notices that some things have changed. "They've gotten faster. I think the kids are crazier. All guts, you know, they release that throttle and they're just hanging on."

Racing is not the only thing different about motorcycling, Magoo reports; the bikers themselves are not really the same. "Some of them are like they used to be, but a lot of them they're changed. They're from all walks of life nowadays. A nicer element nowadays. It's more of a general public sport nowadays than it used to be like in the old 'Wild Ones' and that. Years ago, they had a thing going, there was conflict between clubs. I haven't noticed that lately, no rivalries. When it comes to a large rally like this, it's all neutral territory. They all get along."

Magoo laughs, shakes his head, and describes an additional change in the motorcyling community. "Another thing, years ago I never noticed as many ladies riding their own bikes as nowadays. Jesus, it's overwhelming. I see little women smaller than me riding a bigger bike than I've ever even tried to ride, and I've been riding fifty years at least."

And what does someone who was racing dirt tracks before most of the other rally goers were even born think about all these changes? "I love it," Magoo exclaims happily, "Everything I've heard has always been affirmative, good. I haven't heard anything bad. I haven't seen anything negative. It's a great bunch of people." And it's the people, according to this long-time biker, who make the difference, and who make a rally successful. Sturgis leads the pack. "One good thing about it is folks are exceptionally nice, let me tell you. These are my people. I've been riding for over fifty years, and I love them all, you know, they're my brothers."

MONTY

"I go to all kinds of rallies. All over the United States and Europe. Went to Madrid to a Harley function. I just rented over there."

He paces back and forth outside the car wash, where local high school kids are cleaning bikes as a fundraiser. When they wheel out his white Harley-Davidson Heritage Springer, he points out a few spots they have missed. Eventually, he takes a towel and finishes polishing the bike himself. As a general contractor and owner of his own trucking company in Vancouver, Washington, Monty Center, age 50, is accustomed to having things done right.

Fortunately for Monty, he can temporarily run his business from the road. He's already fielded a dozen phone calls this morning. This allows him the freedom to roam, and his denim vest is covered with pins providing a mini-travelogue of his ventures. "I go to all kinds of rallies. All over. All over the United States and in Europe. Went to Madrid to a Harley function. I just rented over there. I got some friends over there that rent." His travel strategy seems to work, and the people back home don't seem to mind. "They don't care. This is my thing, it's my vacation. They all wish they could come. I pretty much travel by myself. Once in a while my brother goes with me, but pretty much I like to go to these things by myself. I'm on my own schedule."

"The motorcycle lifestyle is basically freedom, and how can somebody take it away?"

Now Monty's schedule has taken him to Sturgis. It's his second time at the rally. "A little wilder, a little dirtier," he says, comparing Sturgis to other rallies. "Some of my favorite events are not here. I like street bike racing in Reno." Even so, Monty feels that, overall, Sturgis is all right. "This is just a good one to come to. It's history. It started here. It's pretty much the oldest biker event around. I think for what it is, it's pretty well controlled. There's a few too many cops, I think they have a few too many restrictions. They've cut it back a lot, but everybody has a good time."

In fact, Sturgis has a lot of what Monty needs to have a good time at a rally. Sturgis has a lot of people. "Basically, I just come here to people watch. I kind of sit back and watch. Make a lot of new friends. That's probably my biggest story, that I make a lot of new friends. There's so many diverse people out here, unless you're closed-minded, you'll make a friend that lives on the street and you'll make a friend that's a doctor, you know." Not only does Monty like to meet new people, he likes to take pictures with them as well. He has collected over 300 photographs of friends he has met at various rallies. Most of them, he admits with a sly grin, are very attractive women.

"I was conceived on the hill, so this is my fiftieth anniversary of being here, really."

While pretty women are more to Monty's liking, he also hangs out with the tough guys as well. "Some of the nicest people that I've ran into here I know are hard-ass, core, bad-to-the-bone bikers. As long as you don't give them a problem, they don't have a problem. Just don't start asking the wrong kinds of questions," he explains, "and that's for anybody and everybody. You don't start talking about their clothes. You don't do that. You don't talk about the patches, or ask them about the patches on their coats. Especially the big bike clubs. You just be cool, and you don't have a problem. You be a smart-ass, and you're going to find yourself probably upside the wall. You can ask for permission, and you can talk about anything you want if they give it to you. But you got to know the ropes. For the most part, if you follow the rules, everybody's pretty cool."

It is obvious looking at and talking to Monty that he is fairly well-to-do. To Monty, there is no contradiction between being a biker and being financially secure. "The motorcycle lifestyle is basically freedom, and how can somebody take it away? Really, just because somebody shows up in a suit doesn't mean that your freedom's gone. I come in a motor home. I got a $160,000 motor home with a trailer, and my Harley sits inside an enclosement. I still have as much fun as the next guy. I have just as much fun as the guy who rides here and camps next to me in a tent."

While Monty doesn't exactly wear a suit to the rally, he does admit that the jeans and sleeveless attire is not his regular look back home. "It just comes out for the rally. Probably here now, looking around, probably fifty percent of the people are kind of that way. They got to go back, and they got to, you know – they got to make a lot of money to buy a brand new Harley. Those things, they're going to start around twenty. A friend of mine just paid forty for one down the road here. You know, you don't do that not working. So they've all got probably pretty good jobs – fifty percent of them. And then you see the ones that probably live to ride their Harley, period. They may spend every cent they make on their Harley. I've met a few of those this time, too."

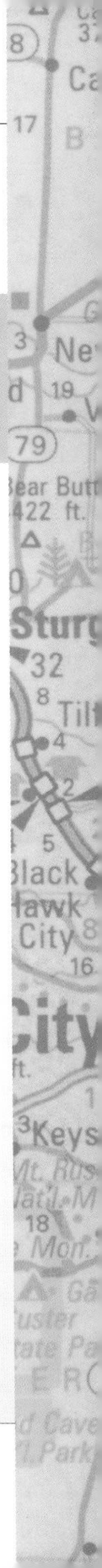

Of course, some of those hard-core riders who spend every cent on their bike tend to complain about the wealthier riders. Looking around the streets, you see plenty of t-shirts making fun of the professionals, or of people who trailer their bikes. "All the t-shirts are nothing but t-shirts. They're just wearing it around. It's no big deal," Monty explains. There are no boundaries, he continues, and everybody – well, almost everybody, belongs. "Anybody who comes here with an attitude shouldn't be here. If they come here with an attitude that they're bigger, meaner, tougher, or better than anybody else, then they should stay home. Other than that, there's nobody that don't belong here."

One thing definitely sets Monty apart from a majority of the upper income bikers. Many of them just recently started riding. Motorcycles have been a part of Monty's entire life, beginning – ironically – here in the Black Hills. "I was conceived on the hill, so this is my fiftieth anniversary of being here, really. My mom and dad, when they got married, they moved to Lead, and Mom was pregnant when they left here. Until I was eight, we didn't have a car – we just had motorcycles with sidecars and stuff. I was riding my dad's Harley '74 when I was twelve years old – driving it. They kind of rode around with the hardcore biker group here, then they moved out to the west coast. They say I was conceived in the back of a motorcycle, so I guess that's probably why…," Monty pauses, shrugs, and concludes, "I can't remember when I didn't have a motorcycle." The look on his face makes one thing clear. However he dresses back in Washington, whatever he owns, and no matter how he got his motorcycle out here, Monty Center has come home.

ORIGINAL
Coors
Bell Bros
So. CaL
8-2000
Sturgis

Papa Smurf

"When I first started coming they'd have the park open down below there. Hell, everybody'd run around naked, starting fires."

In the Dungeon Bar on Main Street, a gaunt man with long dark hair, wearing a tall stovepipe hat and looking a bit like a crazed Victorian undertaker, starts to yell and point to a wiry bearded man standing in the doorway leading out to the alley. "What would you say if I told you I had pictures of him," he hollers, still pointing, "with Rocky Marciano, boxing at Madison Square Garden?" He is referring to Lanny "Papa Smurf" Spaulding, a retired former-boxer who works as a bouncer at the Dungeon during rally week. Papa Smurf nods, leaves his post to take a seat in a nearby booth, and confirms the undertaker's story. "I used to box in the ring. Went twelve years. And Rocky Marciano signed me for eight years. He was a great man. I never lost a fight in twelve years. Then I retired." He looks away, thinking, and chuckles at a memory, "I was pretty – ornery – I'd say. I had a lot of fun doing it. I did it my way. If there's a thing a person wants to do – they do it. You know that."

"I was born and raised in Deadwood," he continues. "I left there in '89, when the gambling first came in, and moved to Oregon – me and my wife. I'm married. Been married for fifteen years. Lived out in Oregon for about a year to two years. Then we moved to Billings for about two years. But we came back for the rally every year." Now, at age 57, Papa Smurf, his wife, and his 2000 personally hand built custom motorcycle, have relocated to Sturgis for good. This is his thirtieth year at the rally.

> "If there's a thing a person wants to do – they do it. You know that."

Over those thirty years, one obvious piece of evidence demonstrates how much the rally has changed. "Oh, God. By the people," Papa Smurf exclaims. As many have noticed, however, more people these days does not mean more trouble than the old days. "Very different. When I first started coming they'd have the park open down below there. Hell, everybody'd run around naked, starting fires." Overall, he believes the changes make the rally more enjoyable. "Seen a lot of people. Met a lot of people. Enjoy a bunch of people. The more they come the better it feels."

"We camp down here with very, very good friends of ours. It's just like a whole, big family reunion once a year. The same people come every year. There's about fifty or sixty of us down there. The yard's full of tents. The driveway's full of bikes. We got to move all the cars and stuff to get the bikes in." He chuckles again. "It's fun."

"Seen a lot of people. Met a lot of people. Enjoy a bunch of people."

The only part that's not fun is how strict the rules have become, and how stringently they are enforced. "We could leave the cops out. They just harass people that they shouldn't. If you do wrong, you do wrong, and you deserve to get picked up. If you don't do wrong, you don't need to be picked up. They hassle you all the time." The biggest injustice, in his eyes, is placed on the women of the rally. "You can't run around with your tits hanging loose," he explains, referring to the fine associated with public flashing. "I know a couple of girls from Utah, they got it. They got busted. Cost'em four hundred bucks. Two hundred dollars apiece." Chuckling, he does the math. "Pay a hundred dollars a tit."

Despite such inconveniences, Papa Smurf believes that the rally will continue to grow. "'Cause it's well known. It's the biggest one around. The rally's free, you know. Who wants to come, comes. I guess that's the way you'd put it. If they're rich or they're poor, if they can make it, make it. It's some great times. That's what it is – one big party. I love it here."

He also loves working at the Dungeon. "I've been working here since they opened the bar. About thirteen years. Thirteen, fourteen, something like that." The bar has a reputation of being a hang out for club members, but rarely is there trouble. Unlike some biker bars, which require gangs to leave their colors at the door, the Dungeon has no such restrictions. "They don't usually wear'em. The Hells Angels, they're about the only ones that wear them. And the BTM's. And the Sundowners. And the…what the heck…Sons of Silence. They mostly wear theirs, so they know who they are."

Still, he insists, there are no problems. "No, we don't get that much trouble. 'Not really. You get your pretty bad ones, and then you've got your good ones." Suddenly, he remembers a story of one of the "bad ones." "I had to deck an old boy downstairs one year…a couple years ago. He was pushing me around and I…," he pauses, and let's out another one of those chuckles, "didn't let him. This guy, he was from California, and he was trying to pick on my wife. He come up behind her and started picking her up, and said 'You're going to California with me.' And I said 'No, that lil' girl ain't going nowhere with you. That's my wife, leave her alone.' And he spun around and

give me a push in the chest…so I decked him." Another chuckle. "I got a hell of a right hook."

Something like that must have scared his wife, maybe even make her want to avoid the rally. "Shit, she loves it. It wouldn't be a rally without her. She's out at the campground right now. She'll probably be out here later. You can't keep her out of the bar." Chuckle again. "I enjoy my wife. I want to go home and she wants to stay, so I got to stay with her." Laughing and shaking his head, he returns to his post by the door.

BUILDERS OF
Pierce
THE FINEST
STURG
2001

"So, we still let the people have their fun, but we kind of keep control so it doesn't get out of hand. It's become safer."

At 38 years old, Ron Koan has a lot of responsibility. He serves as the Fire Chief and Building Official in Sturgis, and will soon be named the Emergency Services Director, covering not only fire safety but emergency medical transport as well. He, along with the other emergency personnel in Sturgis, do their job so well that dignitaries from Salt Lake City have visited the last two rallies to take notes and prepare themselves for the 2002 Olympics. "Which is great for us," Ron explains, "It means a lot to us."

As he did for the Olympic visitors, Ron summarizes his responsibilities during the rally: "During this week, I have code enforcement. I hire ten people to go out on the streets and deal with the vendors as far as being licensed, fire code issues as far as fire retardant tents, tying up their propane tanks, cooking facilities, fire extinguishers, etc., etc. Also keeping vendors from selling on the streets. That's what we do this week in addition, of course, to fighting fires, doing gas spills and oil spills which readily occur during rallies."

"I think we have some of the best motorcycle riding in the nation."

Fortunately, other than the danger of the spills, there has rarely been much of a fire hazard during rally week. There have been no structure fires during the past ten rallies. This year there were three, but only one – an overloaded electrical box in a rental home – was rally related. Ron is proud of his team, adding that their response to this year's structure fires was quick and well handled. Part of that success comes from initiatives Ron has implemented regarding safety regulations. The other part comes from being at the station and prepared. During the regular year, the Sturgis Fire Department is strictly volunteer, but during rally week, it is staffed full-time from noon to midnight daily.

While fires may not take up a lot of the department's time, the vendors certainly do. Most vendors are cooperative, but a few – especially the newcomers – occasionally put up a fuss. "The new vendors that come here have a hard time because the property owners don't relay the ordinances, etc, to the new vendors, unfortunately. We do have a packet that goes out through our management firm…and also through the city. It tells all the county, state, local ordinances and the laws to follow. The vendors that have been coming here for many years, particularly since 1990 when we really transitioned into some enforcement to make this a safer rally – they're easy to deal with. Of course, every year, I would say percentage wise 35% of the vendors are new."

New or old, the vendors collectively cause a little trouble for the locals because they keep showing up earlier and earlier every year, sometimes setting up as many as seven or eight days before the rally begins. Of course, since the vendors show up early, many bikers do as well. "A lot of the people who have been coming for years, they don't want to deal with the crowds. We're finding they're starting to come the week before, tour the hills…and end up back in Sturgis for the beginning of the weekend; get their t-shirts and their trinkets that they normally buy, and then they head home."

And how does the typical Sturgis resident respond to this? "The people are more upset when the vendors show up early than when the bikers show up early. We don't have a big problem with the motorcyclists. A lot of the people in the community like to see them come – it's an entertainment thing for them. We have other events, Calvary Days and so on and so forth throughout the summer, but this is a big end-of-the-summer type of thing that people like to see in general. I think the vendors are the biggest downfall. Not that they're a major problem, but people just hate to see the vendors come. They see maybe the end of summer, that type of thing. And the rally gets stretched out a little longer and longer every year sometimes. And we hear complaints." The only good point seems to be that, because of other events to attend, the vendors don't stick around – they clear out immediately at the rally's end.

"Hopefully they behave themselves a little bit, and don't end up in our jail."

Despite his concerns, Ron remains pretty level-headed about the onslaught of vendors and early attendees. After all, they're showing up because they all love the rally. Though he rides a 2001 Yamaha V-Max himself, and has attended rallies in other states, it is always on "official business" so he can check out their operations and regulations. Those comparisons have shown him why people love his rally, and what makes Sturgis unique. "I think a lot of people come here to ride in the Black Hills. I think we have some of the best motorcycle riding in the nation. This is such an old rally, also. Generations through generations come here. Plus, there's entertainment here and there's a lot of things for people to do. They come to see old friends over the years and, of course, that grows as more people come here."

More people indeed. "We used to have people camping in the park, and that used to be a small crowd of maybe five to twenty thousand people, depending on the year. We had a major transition in 1990 when we went to possibly 300,000 that year, and we haven't had a small rally since. Of course, to keep it safe for our visitors and keep it safe for our citizens, we've had to do some enforcement things such as the vending stands, a little more law enforcement. So, we still let the people have their fun, but we kind of keep control so it doesn't get out of hand. It's become safer. They don't get quite as rowdy as they did in the early 80's, late 70's." He explains that one of the reasons you can have a bigger rally but still have more safety is because of the change in who is attending. "We're getting more professionals. We're getting more affluent people that have money, and they expect to come here and be as safe as they would be in their own home. And for the most part, you can control some of that."

Ron further describes what he calls "The Urban Yuppie," and how this crowd differs from the previous generation. "They're out there. The middle age person that's doing well for themselves. We don't see the rat bikes, I guess, anymore – the guy that barely made it here. That had a good element to it. And by all means those people are very welcome here. But you have the people that drive in here in half million-dollar motor homes, and that's how you see the changing face since the 80's. The 80's – there was the element of the gangs, which was a big element of the rally, and that's now transitioned. They're here, but they're not a big influence on the rally. They're a minor crowd. They always have their little struggles, but I would say in the last four-five years really we haven't had any major confrontations with those people. They don't like the element of the urban yuppies or the people that trailer their motorcycles in. You've got to ride your bike and live the motorcycle spirit, I guess you could say, and a lot of those people don't do that. But, the wanna-be's, the weekend riders, are a big crowd." Ironically, he adds, some of the 1%'ers, the outlaw bikers, are even professional people themselves.

"We don't want the money from the companies. If they want to give us something, give us something tangible."

In addition to dealing with dignitaries, vendors, urban yuppies, and gang members, Ron has one more group he needs to focus on. "A lot of big sponsors want to come here," he explains, leaning against one of his newly donated fire trucks, "Companies help with sponsoring fire engines and ambulances. We don't want the money from the companies. If they want to give us something, give us something tangible that will last us the rest of the year and will be here to help them and the people who come here next year."

With such a cross-section of rally-goers, there remains an unpredictable chemistry in that mix, a mix which emergency personnel keep a close eye on. "There's also that element out there - the unknown element that we have to deal with. It's just a lot of work for us. It's great that the people can come here and enjoy themselves. We hope that people have fun when they come here. Hopefully they behave themselves a little bit, and don't end up in our jail. Hopefully they can be safe and not get injured. We have fatalities every year, and that's an unfortunate thing, but having a crowd of 300,000 – last year estimated at 750,000 – I think we're fortunate. If we had a city that size, we'd probably have more things going on normally than we do with these people coming in to visit this community of 7,000."

Eventually, the rally winds down. The jail empties. The vendors leave, and the fire station goes back to volunteer shifts. Then Ron can rest. "I'm glad to see it go when it does go, to be real honest, 'cause I'm going on two and a half weeks now without a day off. But we get through it. We're on a downhill slide. Occasionally we get a little grumpy, but we don't mean to. But we're long hours. My average hours during this week has been 16-18 hours, and the lack of sleep, and things like that…we all know how that is. But for the most part, it's been a good year. We have a good time. Hopefully the bikers have a good time, and get home safe."

WELCOME!!
COME ON IN!!
PLEASE KEEP
the DOOR
CLOSED!!
BRAVO

SHARON

"When they tell you how good the food is, and how much they've had to eat and how reasonably priced it is, it makes you feel good that you didn't rip them off."

You know the old saying, "When you want something done, ask a busy person." They could have been talking about Sharon Wilson. At age 61, the Black Hawk, SD resident is in her second decade as a Mary Kay beauty consultant, is involved with the local Kiwanis club, spearheads local volunteer activities and fundraisers, and at the moment is coordinating the daily pancake breakfast hosted by Our Lady of the Black Hills Catholic Church, just off the Interstate between Black Hawk and Sturgis. "When I get involved in something, I get involved all the way – hook, line, and sinker. Sometimes, more than I maybe should, but if it needs to be done, I just believe in getting it done."

Though Our Lady of the Black Hills provides the space, Sharon points out, the Kiwanis actually host the breakfast. "And now this year we've added an Eagle Scout and his project. He's building a playground up on the Lutheran church's land that they're letting him put it on. We're buying his material, he's doing the work. And the other portion of our money...we took on a big project to build a sidewalk along Peaceful Pines Road, which is down a mile from this church. That road was very narrow and had no shoulders, and had school kids walking on it. It was very dangerous. So we took on the project of getting a sidewalk built. We raised the money; the National Guard did our work. The sidewalk's done, and the driveways will go in next week, and it just makes you feel...," Sharon pauses, looking for the right words, "every minute of this week is worth it because of that project."

Good thing each minute is worth it, because those minutes add up to hours each and every day. "Well, we get here early in the morning and we cook our sausages and mix up our pancakes, and put out our butters and jellies, and make our coffee. And then we're ready to start feeding people. And we have people come through the door at 7 o'clock. We feed pancakes and sausage until noon. Sometimes it's slow, sometimes it's steady. We'll have six or eight or ten come through the door at once. We don't make pancakes ahead and stack them at a steam table, 'cause we think they get tough. So, we tell them to get their coffee and their juice, their eating utensils, and we'll bring them their fresh, hot pancakes off the griddle. It's great having the Scouts 'cause then they serve them." As if getting through each day isn't enough, Sharon is already planning for the future. "We're thinking next year we're probably going to add biscuits and gravy to our menu, because we've had guys in here – what

have we done this now, five days – and we've had guys here every morning. I think they might be getting a little tired of pancakes, but we appreciate the fact that they're coming back."

Whatever Sharon serves, she's committed to making sure people get a good deal for their money. "And our prices, I don't know if they're the least, but I think they are close to being the least costly for a meal. My feeling on it, and our Kiwanis Club's feeling on it, is those people don't have to get ripped off when they come out here. We don't have to try and get rich off of that this week. And so our price is $3.50, and that's for all they can eat pancakes and sausage, and a juice or a milk, and coffee. That's probably a pretty reasonable meal." Sharon leans forward, and says in a conspiratorial tone, "We've checked out prices 'down the way,' and they're more than ours."

"We have about 125 a day," Sharon says, describing her typical day of customers. "We could feed more. Most of them are really friendly biker guys and gals. You come out when you get a break and ask them where they're from, and about the weather. It's fun seeing the guys come back day after day. They start to get to know you, and they're spreading the word, too. When they tell you how good the food is, and how much they've had to eat and how reasonably priced it is, it makes you feel good that you didn't rip them off."

"They're just such genuine, nice people. You know, you almost would trust them with your life."

"I had a group sit back here this morning in the dark. I had not turned those lights on back there," she says, pointing to the back half of the dimly lit church basement where the meals are served, "Then a lady in the kitchen said, 'Don't you think you should turn on the lights?' So I came down to those guys. There was six of them there. I said, 'So, guys, we're worried in the kitchen that you're sitting down here in the dark.' 'Oh,' they said, 'No, we like it. It's good for our eyes. Besides, we look so bad, nobody else should be looking at us.' So I left them in the dark."

> "When I get invoved in something, I get involved all the way – hook, line, and sinker."

In addition to a good deal on pancakes, Our Lady of the Black Hills offers other benefits for road-weary motorcyclists. It has air conditioning, and a lobby area filled with couches. "We've had three or four guys, for two or three days in a row, after they've eaten here, they've gone out there and taken a nap. You'll have a bunch a guys sitting in here, and I'll say to them, 'Look, you guys don't have to leave. If you were in a restaurant, you'd have to get out, but we've got room. You can just sit and visit where it's cool.'"

Not surprisingly, Sharon's hospitality doesn't end at the church doors. She has a history of going out of her way to make rally-goers comfortable. "My husband and I were putting up the last signs for the food last year, and I encountered four people sitting at the campground down here. I stopped and told them about the pancake breakfast, and one of them said 'Did we know where they could camp that night?' The two guys were going on to North Dakota, but the two women were needing a place to stay, so we said, 'Would you like to stay with us?' So the guys got in the car and went to Minot that night, 'cause they had business up there, and the women came and stayed with us. I didn't have any qualms about taking home absolute strangers, because they looked safe, they looked nice - -and they were."

Sharon's motivation for helping them out was a simple one. "'Cause I love the Black Hills, so to make them feel welcomed in the Black Hills." Even though she loves the hills and the rally, she really doesn't make an effort to go into town. She only goes in to conduct business or, no surprise, to show hospitality to visitors. "We went there last year, because we had company come. And so we took my cousin and his wife down on Thursday. He was just open-mouthed. The year before my brother and his family came, and we went on an afternoon. We haven't been there this year. Now I have to go to Sturgis this afternoon to pay my sales tax on my sales here, so who knows, I may walk through it a little bit. But otherwise, no, that's not something that we usually do. By the time you get through this six days, seven days, and I'm here everyday from the start to the finish, I'm happy to go home in the afternoon and put my feet up. If it cools tomorrow, there isn't anything to say that we might not go, but I just don't feel too excited about it."

"It's gotten bigger. It's gotten more expensive. It's gotten lots more vendors."

A couple of reasons that Sharon avoids the downtown area are the crowds and the sellers. "It's gotten bigger. It's gotten more expensive. It's gotten lots more vendors. I don't how they can make that many more different kinds of shirts and different kinds of things to sell, but they keep doing it." Still, it's a fair trade-off. There may be more people and booths, but the atmosphere is friendlier than in the past. "It's a little tamer. When it first was going on, it could get rough in Sturgis. There were campgrounds that women had to raise up and show under their shirts before they could get in the gate. And there were campgrounds that nobody would go to, except this one certain group would go there. There were some hardcore groups. I think those hardcore groups are still here, but I think they're a little more mellow."

Even though she doesn't get to town often, Sharon has some good insights about the changes in the biker culture. "Lots and lots of these guys are doctors and dentist and lawyers that have let their beards grow for a week or two. This is their vacation. They love riding their motorcycles, and they go home, shave off their beards, and go back to work. You hear them. They kid about how they'll grow their beard for a month, and they come to the rally, and then go back to being Joe Cool in their dentist chair. One of the members of our Kiwanis Club that helped get our group started – we've just been in business four years – he's a pretty hardcore biker. His comment is, he hates these Yuppies. He thinks the Yuppies have ruined the motorcycle rally, because he just would like it to be 'motorcycle people.' But, it wouldn't be nearly as big or as successful, or as much money coming in, if you didn't have the Yuppies come. You know, there isn't any getting around it."

Sharon's hardcore Kiwanis friend isn't the only local who doesn't like all the people flocking to the region. "Some of them just hate it." But, like Sharon with her pancake breakfast, they know there's no way getting around it, and they make the best of it. "A lot of them, they rent their basement and they rent rooms, so a lot of them they make money from it. I know a lady from the bank that last year, they moved to town. She still had work and her husband still had work, so they moved in with their in-laws and they rented out their whole house. I've heard people say that when they come home that their houses are cleaner than when they'd left them. Their yard has been mowed and watered, and all the beds are cleaned, and the refrigerator is full of food. Those kind of people you'd love to rent to. I don't know of anybody that's had any bad experience renting to anyone. So, I'd say for a majority of the people, it's okay."

Basically, Sharon feels that those who complain about the rally are the type of folks who will complain about most anything, including her pet projects. "There's always some nay-sayers. There's some people that complained about my new sidewalk over there. Well, if they don't like the way we did it, then they could have done it." Sharon shares a few thoughts about what she might like to say to those complainers, then, looking around, she stops abruptly. "But I haven't said it yet."

STACY

"I think what's left unseen is more sexy than exposing it all. It leaves more for the imagination"

What's the first thing you notice about Stacy Schweigel? The platinum mane, pouring out of a black leather hair wrap? The sultry eyes? The body glitter? The nose ring? Well, sure, you notice all those things, but c'mon, what you really notice are those tattoos.

The 36-year-old mother of two teenage girls (who think Mom is "way cool") owns and operates a ranch with her husband in Absarokee, Montana, and has been collecting the tattoos for half her life. "This started when I was eighteen years old, with a very little one. And it's just been something that's been an addiction, I guess you want to call it, a fascination of mine. I don't know when it will end." Unlike some tattoo aficionados, who meticulously plan their tattoo murals in advance, Stacy has no actual grand plan or design to her body art. "It's just whatever I feel at the time. Maybe the mood I'm in or the situation I'm in; where I'm at in my life."

"It probably tells a story, too," Stacy adds. Looking down, she laughs, "Oh, there's probably a few stories. You could probably call them memories." What those memories are, however, Stacy is not sharing. What she does share is that she won't be adding to her collection here in Sturgis. Not just any tattoo artist gets to add to the unfolding story-line on Stacy's skin. "I've got someone back home that I'm very faithful to. I've got some from Hawaii, but the rest are from Montana. When I find an artist I pretty much stay with that particular one."

There may be no tattoos for Stacy in Sturgis, but there's plenty for her to do. "I like to people watch, so I find it quite interesting. That's probably the main

reason why I come, to look at all the characters." This is her second time at the rally and, though she thinks Sturgis is a "rat race," it's still worth the trip to "be a part of something that's so big. People come from everywhere, even overseas, to be here. I think it's interesting that different walks of life can show up here. It's pretty awesome."

"When I find an artist I pretty much stay with that particular one."

She and her husband take in the usual attractions, like Mount Rushmore (which Stacy refers to as "the heads"), and they still plan to hit a few of the hot spots like the Full Throttle Saloon and the Buffalo Chip campground. So far, "It's all been good." Most important, Stacy just got her bike, a 1995 Harley-Davidson Dyna, so she's been "shopping for accessories." After all, what's a Harley-Davidson without accessories?

"Everybody wants to show off their bike," Stacy explains, especially in a place like Sturgis. "It's heard about across the country. I think part of this is to show off your bike and be a part of something that is a big event for everybody." And when Stacy says the event is for everybody, she means everybody. "Whether you're a lawyer or you work with your hands doing construction, I think it should be open to all. I don't think there should be any boundaries. If you start making boundaries, then you lose the uniqueness about it. You know, if you have one type of people that can go, what's the fun in that?"

One of the boundaries that has definitely gone by the wayside is the old taboo about women who ride their own motorcycles. Stacy has crossed over that line, and enjoys every minute of it. "I feel independent, and I like that. It's like a challenge. I rode a dirt bike when I was a kid, so I knew I could do it. I was just afraid of the congestion, the traffic, the heavier bike. I like it. I like the freedom and the independence that it gives me."

So, she rides her own Harley. Has tattoos. Wears leather. One has to wonder if this is how she looks and acts back home at the ranch. Stacy says it is. "More or less me all the time. Maybe it's not leathers all the time, but I dress to be fun. I have the tattoos, of course, to show them. I don't hide anything."

Suddenly, remembering the city she is in, she changes her tone. "I don't overexpose, either, as far as under dressing," she confirms, just so there's no misunderstanding. "I just feel that's for home."

"I have the tattoos, of course, to show them. I don't hide anything."

"To a certain extent I guess I'm an exhibitionist because of the tattoos, and that's why I get them. I get enjoyment out of it and I like to show them. But as far as showing any private parts of my body, I don't agree with that. I think what's left unseen is more sexy than exposing it all. It leaves more for the imagination." If that's the case, it doesn't always take much imagination in Sturgis.

"My husband says that the ones that are doing it are the ones who should be covering up. They're doing it for attention. Maybe that's what a lot of this is about. People want attention. I'm a little bit more private than that. To each their own. I'm not going to criticize a girl if she's half-naked. Maybe I might make a comment to my husband – 'That's a little much' or 'That's uncalled for' or whatever. I keep to myself about that. I don't make any waves with people about it. But it's not anything I would be doing."

Obviously, Stacy is comfortable with herself and her decisions. Her public image and what she shares is done with pride, and not out of some need for approval. She wishes others could be more like that. "People should be themselves, whatever walk of life they are. If you've got something to be proud of and you want to show it – be proud of it and show. Don't care what other people think."

Good philosophy. As her daughters would say, "Way cool."

DAVIDSON
LIFE
FULL
Important

STEVE

"You can talk to anybody, whether it be somebody from one of the outlaw biker gangs to police officers that are working the barricades in the evening."

Want an interview? Steve Nyhaug gets right down to business. "I'm a 49-year-old police lieutenant. Married to the same woman for 28 years. Two grown children. I enjoy riding motorcycles. This is my sixth trip to Sturgis. It's an opportunity to spend time with friends that have a similar interest. I enjoy riding in the Black Hills. I come out at least twice a year."

That just about covers it, right? Other than knowing his beat, Sioux Falls, SD, and his ride, a 2000 Harley-Davidson Road King, it first appears that this is all the information Lt. Nyhaug intends to convey. With a little prodding, however, one discovers that Steve is one of the things that Sturgis promoters love the most. He is a fan. "It's a great place to ride motorcycles. I think that's one of the reasons Sturgis is as large as it is. I got friends who think I'm nuts for coming out here, and putting up with all the crowds, and putting up with all the hassles. But, for me, it's kind of a break from what I normally do. In my job, the expectations are a little different than the week you're out here. And it's just kind of a place to come and relax, have a good dinner, and good riding."

Oh, and there's one other reason Steve likes the rally. "The people watching. The numbers of people from all over the world that find the desire to make that commitment to come here. It's the different kinds of motorcycles. The different kinds of people. It's meeting people from all over – all over the country and all over the world. It's the granddaddy of them all." At this point, a little bit of cop shows through, as Steve comments on the safety of rally-goers. "Sturgis is a time period where, during the rally, you really have to be careful because of the crowds and the number of motorcycles on the road. Early in the summer, before schools out, first weekend after Memorial Day, we come out and you virtually have the hills to yourself."

Other than a few South Dakota H.O.G. (Harley Owners Group) rallies, Steve hasn't been to other rallies like Daytona or Laconia. But he can sure tell you a lot about this one. "This is the 61st year, so it's something that's grown. The first year I came out here, in '96, I think there was 150,000-175,000 people. Last year there was 650 – the estimate was – thousand people that found this the destination spot. It's quite a unique experience." In fact, Steve credits – or blames – all the changes that have taken place in Sturgis to the sheer numbers of people that show up. "The changes are all due to that. Wherever you go and whatever you do, you got to stand in line and wait. And that's really the annoying part about it – the fact that it's not nearly as small and user-friendly, so to speak, as it once was. It's more difficult, but you just know that going into it, and you just accept it before you ever come. You try to condition yourself to have patience to deal with the numbers, and then everything's all right."

"It's meeting people from all over – all over the country and all over the world."

Some might think that, because of the crowds, Sturgis ought to go back to its old ways, catering simply to the hard-core motorcyclists. Not Steve Nyhaug. "No, I think it's everybody that enjoys motorcycling; enjoys riding their motorcycle in gorgeous country; enjoys the friendly people of the state of South Dakota. The 'us' and 'them' may exist elsewhere, but it doesn't exist in downtown Sturgis." To this, the gruff looking police officer adds, "You can talk to anybody, whether it be somebody from one of the outlaw biker gangs to police officers that are working the barricades in the evening. You can walk up and talk to virtually anybody."

Of course, talking to Steve might be a little intimidating to some. With his husky frame, patriotic skull cap, and general air of authority, people might not always recognize the enthusiastic South Dakota-spokesperson underneath those dark glasses. At least we know it's not an act. The look is all Steve.

"Generally, it's the person I take back home. The person I am at home is the person that's out at Sturgis. I don't try to be something that I'm not, for anybody. I've been fairly successful being who I am, and I don't see a need to change it. There's no reason to. You're accepted. If you want to visit with people you can, people will accept you for who you are. And there's no need to try to put on a front and become something you're not. Most people that do that aren't very successful at it, because their real them shows through."

Whether its real or whether it's a front, one question remains. Does it have to be a Harley-Davidson? "No, absolutely not. This year, I'm out with a group of five fellas. Four of us are from Sioux Falls, and then a friend out of

Minneapolis. Three of us ride Harleys, one rides a Victory that's made by Polaris, and the other rides an Excelsior-Henderson. No, it doesn't have to be a Harley. People don't make fun of the motorcycle you ride as long as you're enjoying doing that on two wheels."

Of course, whatever you're riding doesn't always guarantee that it will be fun. Steve vividly remembers his most dangerous Sturgis experience. "One year, when we came out here, we started to ride out from Rapid – and by the time we got to Sturgis it was raining so hard we didn't even pull in – we just wanted to get to the cabin. We got off the interstate at Highway 85, the four-lane into Deadwood, and before we got to Deadwood it started to hail. And later on that night, after we'd gotten to the cabin and gotten warmed up, and went back into Deadwood for a bite to eat, the snowplows had to come out and scrape the hail off the roads. That was an experience that, when you're riding a distance like that, you'll never forget."

Just as Sturgis is unforgettable, Steve observes, it is also sometimes unexplainable. "If you had to try to explain the experience to somebody that wasn't here…" he muses, then continues with an example, "At the 2000 rally, the 60th anniversary, the first rally of the millennium, my dad's cousin's husband came to Sioux Falls from Oslo, Norway. I was already in the hills. He brought my pickup and trailer out. I met him. We hooked up just like we had said we would, and I spent the rest of the week with him. And he had absolutely such a great time. And he was accepted. He spoke English – broken English – but he is an educated man. He's an accountant in Norway. And he absolutely had a ball. He says he's coming back. And it's those kinds of experiences that you have, I guess…trying to explain it to him when we conversed back and forth by e-mail, it was very difficult. He had no idea. He got here, and he was absolutely fascinated. We stayed until 11-12 o'clock every night. He just sat and watched: watched the people and watched what was going on. You know, he'd heard about it and read about it on the Internet…but until you get here and take a look for yourself, it's a difficult place to explain."

VICKI

"I'm such a loner when I ride that I don't think I would be very happy belonging to a big group. I love being by myself."

"I LOVE to ride my motorcycle," exclaims Vicki Pearce, a 47-year-old small business owner from the state of Washington. She must really mean it, considering that she rode her 2001 Harley-Davidson Road Glide completely solo for 1200 miles to get to the rally. "This is my seventh time coming to Sturgis, and my third time riding out here by myself – as in nobody with me. It's just a big adventure every time."

"Well, basically, it's not the event as much as it is the ride to get here. For me, it's a real feeling of freedom. I have to be very social in my job, so it's a time when I kind of go inside myself. In fact, this time at Sturgis I think I've been more social than I ever have been before. On the way, when I'm riding by myself, even at gas stops I don't talk to anybody. I'm such a loner when I ride that I don't think I would be very happy belonging to a big group. I love being by myself. And that's unusual; a lot of people enjoy getting together with a big group and riding, but I've found that I don't have to worry about when anybody else has to go to the bathroom, or when anybody wants to eat. I can just be on my own rhythm, and I really enjoy it. It's just sort of a spiritual time and a quiet time for me."

And Sturgis isn't the only rally that Vicki visits on her spiritual quests. She's attended the Laughlin River Run, and rallies in Hollister and Reno. Sturgis, however, holds a special place in her heart. "There's just something exciting about coming to the big daddy of the rallies. You just see so many different types of people. People that you just know are probably schoolteachers and doctors at home. And then you see hardcore, old school biker types. You see more women riders here than I do at most rallies, and that's always nice. I guess if you're a people watcher, this is the place to do it. And riding through the Black Hills is beautiful. I enjoy that, too."

And what about those schoolteachers and doctors? Vicki's opinion is clear. "A lot of old school bikers are very upset about what they call the Yuppie bikers. I'm not upset about them. In my exposure to those kinds of people, some of them really get a passion for it, and anybody that has a passion for any kind of a sport or activity, has the right and deserves to be able to participate in it. And those that don't develop a passion for it, they quit really soon. Who's to say they shouldn't, or cant?" Of course, Vicki does feel strongly about one habit often attributed to Yuppies. "The thing that bothers me are the trailers. You know, if it's all about riding motorcycles, then ride it. I hate to see people trailering. There's always a certain number of people that need to trailer because of their circumstances. But if it's a motorcycle rally then, for godsakes, ride your motorcycle to it."

"I think the weirdest thing I saw was a guy with eyeballs tattooed on each cheek of his butt."

And as long as you are riding that motorcycle, it doesn't matter what brand it is. "I think if you love to ride, ride what you feel comfortable riding." But for Vicki, it has to be a Harley-Davidson. "For me it does. There's a certain mystique about it. There's a culture involved in it. I ride a really big bike. It's a touring bike because I travel a lot on it, and it's just what I love. I love the feel of it, I love the sound of it, love the culture that goes along with it. For me there wouldn't be anything else."

So Vicki rides her Harley. And rides. And rides. And as she does, she works hard to add a little creativity to the experience. "Every year that I come I try to do something a little bit different. So, last year, I tried to stay in motels with a log cabin theme the whole way out. You know, silly things like that." One of her creative touches was the year she stood on Main Street day after day, just to take pictures of the most unusual things she could find. "And there's no shortage of them. I think the weirdest thing I saw was a guy with eyeballs tattooed on each cheek of his butt. He had to wear his pants quite low so his butt crack was showing, and I chased him down and said, 'Can I take a picture of your butt?' And he let me, but – you know – he was pretty strange."

"The first few years I came here I stayed in what's called the Southside campgrounds by the helicopter pad. And it's a pretty mellow campground; they don't have bands. And so I decided the last couple of years to kind of branch out and do some different things and experience different things, 'cause otherwise I'm here every year and it's the same old thing. And I try to go to a different place and area each year as well. I never set anything up before; I just show up here and do whatever. Last year, I stayed in a tent in someone's backyard, and that was something really different." This year is no exception. "I'm staying at Glencoe. And Glencoe has a reputation for being a really wild campground - a lot of nudity. They have what they call the titty-parade every evening. I will not be participating," Vicki announces, "but I'll probably watch."

Though she doesn't participate in the spectacle, Vicki has no problem with the nudity or the skimpy clothing that some women wear. "Oh, I just think people are having a good time, and that's fine." The atmosphere of fun, she explains, is what makes it okay. It would be different if she felt the women were subjecting themselves to danger. "One thing I will say as a woman, I have never, ever, ever felt unsafe here. The worse thing that anyone has ever even said to me was in a bar a couple years ago and it wasn't even bad, it was funny. I was waiting for my husband. One guy sat down with his friends and he looked at me and he goes, 'Well, you're kind of good looking. I'd do ya'. And that was the worse thing anybody's said to me. It's just not that bad."

"And men, bless their hearts, I'm not a man-hater at all, but men say the stupidest things to me."

Not only does Vicki feel safe and accepted as a woman in general, she also feels right at home as a woman who rides. "Everybody has the right to ride. Motorcycling and bikers to me has always been about acceptance. And so if you're going to be all about freedom and acceptance, you can't decide not to allow other people their freedom, or accept that they're doing their thing." One of the many freedoms Vicki enjoys is the freedom not to drink. "I am a clean and sober girl. It doesn't create a problem here or anywhere. And it's not because I'm a prude – it's just because I hate the hangovers."

In some respects, Vicki is the ultimate female rider. Independent. Creative. Tolerant. Sober. One must be careful, however, to remember that Vicki as a person is more than just Vicki as a rider. She explains, "This is what I do because I love to do it. It's not who I am. And I think that's the most common mistake that people make about me. It is very much a part of my life, but it is not who I am. And so I get a lot of stereotypical comments. And men, bless their hearts, I'm not a man-hater at all, but men say the stupidest things to me. For instance, I pulled up to a motel recently in Washington when I was going somewhere, and I was alone, and these guys turned around and they said, 'So, how many in your group?' What group? Can you see anybody else? And I get comments like, 'Did you ride that here all by yourself?' or just 'Did you ride that?' Well, yeah, I just got off of it…I didn't push it. Some people say kind of silly things."

Well, strangers may not understand Vicki and her solo riding on a huge motorcycle, but those closest to her certainly do. "People that really know me think it's fabulous. My parents, my family, they all think it's just great. My husband rides, too, but he belongs to a motorcycle club so he was on a trip right before this so couldn't come with me. He has total confidence in my ability. We often now travel separately, but he's totally supportive of it and thinks it's wonderful." Good thing, too, since it sounds like solo-Vicki has many a solitary journey ahead. "I don't even like to ride with my husband," she jokes, "because he doesn't go very fast….sorry, honey"

NOTES

1 Ann Ferrar. Hear Me Roar: Women, Motorcycles, and the Rapture of the Road. (North Conway, New Hampshire: Whitehorse Press, 2000): 131.

2 Hunter S. Thompson. Hell's Angels: A Strange and Terrible Saga. (New York, NY: Ballantine Books, 1966): 66-67.

3 Ralph "Sonny" Barger, with Keith and Kent Zimmerman. Hell's Angel: The Life and Times of Sony Barger and the Hell's Angels Motorcycle Club. (New York, NY: William Morrow, 2000): 7.

4 Barger, 8.

5 Brock Yates. Outlaw Machine: Harley-Davidson and the Search for the American Soul. (New York: Broadway Books, 1999): 172.

6 Timothy Egan. "Hell on Wheels, With a Few Creaky Parts." The New York Times on the Web. (2001, July 12): Available at http://www.nytimes.com.

7 Yates, 183.

8 If you really want to see some interesting biography/photography works about motorcycling, check out these books.

Martin Dixson (Photographs) and Greg Tate (Essay). Brooklyn Kings: New York City's Black Bikers. (New York, NY: powerHouse Books, 2000).

Rich Remsberg. Riders for God: The Story of a Christian Motorcycle Gang. (Urbana and Chicago: University of Illinois Press, 2000).

10 Yates, xvii.

11 Yates, 159a.

12 Rich Teerlink and Lee Ozley. More Than a Motorcycle: The Leadership Journey at Harley-Davidson. (Boston, MA: Harvard Business School Press, 2000): 2.

13 Garri Garripoli. Tao of the Ride: Motorcycles and the Mechanics of the Soul. (Deerfield Beach, FL: Health Communications, Inc., 1999): 74-75.

14 Garripoli, 82.